Vietnam Travel Guide

by Alex Pitt

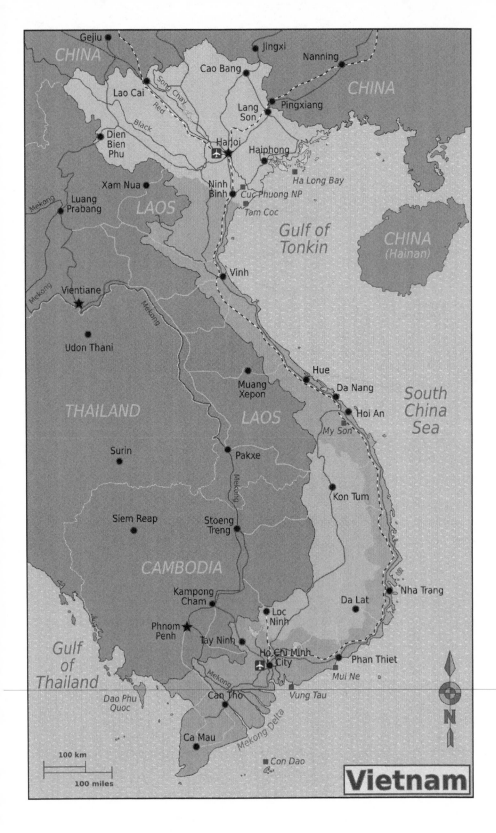

2

Table of Contents

Quick facts about Vietnam

Location: South East Asia

Full country name: Socialist Republic of Vietnam

Area: 329,566 sq. km (128, 527 square miles).

Population: Over 83 million (Growth Rate 1.2%).

Capital city: Hanoi (population 4 million).

People: 85% ethnic Vietnamese, 3% ethnic Chinese, also Khmer, Cham (a remnant of the once great Indianised Champa Kingdom) and members of some 55 ethno-linguistic groups.

Languages: Vietnamese, French, Chinese, English and a variety of Mon-Khmer and Malayo-Polynesian local dialects.

Religions: Buddhism is the principal religion but there are also sizeable Taoist, Confucian, Hoa Hao, Cao Dai, Muslim and Christian minorities.

Vietnam is the largest exporter of cashews in the world, and the second largest exporter of rice.

Instead of bells, traditional gongs are used to call the Vietnamese children to school.

Although Vietnam is a developing country, it has a literacy rate of 94%.

Among all developing countries, Vietnam has one of the lowest unemployment rates.

You can find a B52 American Bomber Wreck in Vietnam's West Lake.

An estimated ten million motor bikes travel on the roads of Vietnam every day.

Ruou ran (snake wine), a Vietnamese specialty of rice wine with a pickled snake inside, allegedly can cure any sickness.

The most common surname in Vietnam is Nguyen.

The Vietnamese keep potbelly pigs as pets.

The Vietnamese language has six different tones. A change in tone changes the meaning of the word. This makes their language somewhat difficult to learn.

The Socialist Republic of Vietnam, the Capital of which is Hanoi, is one of the world's last surviving one-party Communist states. It shares land borders with China, Laos and Cambodia. Vietnam comprises over 330,000 square kilometers, with more than 3400km of coastline.

Vietnam has a population of ninety million, of which around seventy percent live in the countryside, giving Vietnam some of the highest rural population densities in Southeast Asia. Over half the people are under 25 years old and thirteen percent belong to one of the many ethnic minority groups.

Over half of the Vietnamese population earn their living from agriculture. The average per capita income hovers around $1000 a year, though many people survive on less than $2 a day.

During the last decade the Vietnamese economy has grown at over seven percent a year. Vietnam has transformed itself from being a rice-importer before 1986 to become the world's second largest rice-exporter after Thailand. The percentage of households living in poverty has fallen from seventy percent in the 1980s to around ten percent today.

Vietnam is home to a tremendous diversity of plant and animal life, including some of the world's rarest species, a number of which have only been discovered in the last few years. The Asiatic black bear, Sarus crane and Golden-headed langur are just some of the endangered species maintaining a toehold in the forests and wetlands of Vietnam.

History

Vietnam has a history as rich and evocative as anywhere on the planet. Sure, the American War in Vietnam captured the attention of the West, but centuries before that Vietnam was scrapping with the Chinese, the Khmers, the Chams and the Mongols. Vietnamese civilization is as sophisticated as that of its mighty northern neighbor China, from where it drew many of its influences under a thousand-year occupation. Later came the French and the humbling period of colonialism from which Vietnam was not to emerge until the second half of the 20th century. The Americans were simply the last in a long line of invaders who had come and gone through the centuries and, no matter what was required or how long it took, they too would be vanquished. If only the planners back in Washington had paid just a little more attention to the history of this very proud nation, then Vietnam might have avoided the trauma and tragedy of a horribly brutal war.

Visitors to Vietnam can't help but notice that the same names pop up again and again on the streets of every city and town. These are Vietnam's national heroes who, over the last 2000 years, have led the country in its repeated expulsions of foreign invaders and whose exploits have inspired subsequent generations of patriots.

The early days

Recent archaeological finds suggest that the earliest human habitation of northern Vietnam was about 500, 000 years ago. Neolithic cultures were romping around the same area just 10, 000 years ago and engaged in primitive agriculture as early as 7000 BC. The sophisticated Bronze Age Dong Son culture, which is famous for its drums, emerged sometime around the 3rd century BC.

From the 1st to 6th centuries AD, southern Vietnam was part of the Indianised Cambodian kingdom of Funan – famous for its refined art and architecture. Known as Nokor Phnom to the Khmers, this kingdom was centered on the walled city of Angkor Borei, near modern-day Takeo. The Funanese constructed an elaborate system of canals both for transportation and the irrigation of rice. The principal port city of Funan was Oc-Eo in the Mekong Delta and archaeological excavations here tell us of contact between Funan and China, Indonesia, Persia and even the Mediterranean.

The Hindu kingdom of Champa emerged around present-day Danang in the late 2nd century AD. Like Funan, it adopted Sanskrit as a sacred language and borrowed heavily from Indian art and culture. By the 8th century Champa had expanded southward to include what is now Nha Trang and Phan Rang. The Cham were a feisty bunch who conducted raids along the entire coast of Indochina, and thus found themselves in a perpetual state of war with the Vietnamese to the north and the Khmers to the south. Ultimately this cost them their kingdom, as they found themselves squeezed between two great powers. Check out some brilliant sculptures in the Museum of Cham Sculpture in Danang.

1000 Years of Chinese Domination

The Chinese conquered the Red River Delta in the 2nd century BC. In the following centuries, large numbers of Chinese settlers, officials and scholars moved south to impose a centralized state system on the Vietnamese.

Needless to say, local rulers weren't very happy about this and in the most famous act of resistance, in AD 40, the Trung Sisters (Hai Ba Trung) rallied the people, raised an army and led a revolt that sent the Chinese governor fleeing. The sisters proclaimed themselves queens of an independent Vietnam. In AD 43 the Chinese counterattacked and, rather than suffer the ignominy of surrender, the Trung Sisters threw themselves into the Hat Giang River. There were numerous small-scale rebellions against Chinese rule – which was characterized by tyranny, forced labor and insatiable demands for tribute – from the 3rd to 6th centuries, but all were crushed.

During this era, Vietnam was a key port of call on the sea route between China and India. The Chinese introduced Confucianism, Taoism and Mahayana Buddhism to Vietnam, while the Indians brought Theravada Buddhism. Monks carried with them the scientific and medical knowledge of these two great civilizations and Vietnam was soon producing its own great doctors, botanists and scholars.

The early Vietnamese learned much from the Chinese, including the construction of dikes and irrigation works. These innovations helped make rice the 'staff of life', and paddy agriculture remains the foundation of the Vietnamese way of life to this day. As food became more plentiful the population expanded, forcing the Vietnamese to seek new lands. The ominous Truong Son Mountains prevented westward expansion, so the Vietnamese headed south.

Liberation from China

In the early 10th century the Tang dynasty in China collapsed. The Vietnamese seized the initiative and launched a long overdue revolt against Chinese rule in Vietnam. In 938 AD popular patriot Ngo Quyen finally vanquished the Chinese armies at a battle on the Bach Dang River, ending 1000 years of Chinese rule. However, it was not the last time the Vietnamese would tussle with their mighty northern neighbor.

From the 11th to 13th centuries, Vietnamese independence was consolidated under the enlightened emperors of the Ly dynasty, founded by Ly Thai To. During the Ly dynasty, many enemies launched attacks on Vietnam, among them the Chinese, the Khmer and the Cham but all were repelled. Meanwhile, the Vietnamese continued their expansion southwards and slowly but surely began to consolidate control of the Cham kingdom.

Mongol warrior Kublai Khan completed his conquest of China in the mid-13th century. For his next trick, he planned to attack Champa and demanded the right to cross Vietnamese territory. The Vietnamese refused, but the Mongol hordes – all 500, 000 of them – pushed ahead, seemingly invulnerable. However, they met their match in the legendary general Tran Hung Dao; he defeated them in the battle of Bach Dang River, one of the most celebrated scalps among many the Vietnamese have taken.

China bites back

The Chinese seized control of Vietnam again in the early 15th century, carting off the national archives and some of the country's intellectuals to China – an irreparable loss to Vietnamese civilization. The Chinese controlled much of the country from 1407, imposing a regime of heavy taxation and slave labor. The poet Nguyen Trai (1380–1442) wrote of this period:

Were the water of the Eastern Sea to be exhausted, the stain of their ignominy could not be washed away; all the bamboo of the Southern Mountains would not suffice to provide the paper for recording all their crimes.

Le Loi enters the scene

In 1418 wealthy philanthropist Le Loi sparked the Lam Son Uprising, travelling the countryside to rally the people against the Chinese. Upon victory in 1428, Le Loi declared himself Emperor Le Thai To, the first in the long line of the Le dynasty. To this day, Le Loi is riding high in the Top Ten of the country's all-time national heroes.

Following Le Loi's victory over the Chinese, Nguyen Trai, a scholar and Le Loi's companion in arms, wrote his infamous Great Proclamation (Binh Ngo Dai Cao). Guaranteed to fan the flames of nationalism almost six centuries later, it articulated Vietnam's fierce spirit of independence:

Our people long ago established Vietnam as an independent nation with its own civilization. We have our own mountains and our own rivers, our own customs and traditions, and these are different from those of the foreign country to the north…We have sometimes been weak and sometimes powerful, but at no time have we suffered from a lack of heroes.

Le Loi and his successors launched a campaign to take over Cham lands to the south, wiping the kingdom of Champa from the map, and parts of eastern Laos were forced to kowtow to the might of the Vietnamese.

The coming of the Europeans

The first Portuguese sailors came ashore at Danang in 1516 and were soon followed by a proselytizing party of Dominican missionaries. During the following decades the Portuguese began to trade with Vietnam, setting up a commercial colony alongside those of the Japanese and Chinese at Faifo (present-day Hoi An). The Catholic Church eventually had a greater impact on Vietnam than on any country in Asia except the Philippines (which was ruled by the Spanish for 400 years).

Lording it over the people

In a dress rehearsal for the tumultuous events of the 20th century, Vietnam found itself divided in half through much of the 17th and 18th centuries. The powerful Trinh Lords were later Le kings who ruled the North. To the south were the Nguyen Lords, who feigned tribute to the kings of the north but carried on like an independent kingdom. The powerful Trinh failed in their persistent efforts to subdue the Nguyen, in part because their Portuguese weaponry was far inferior to the Dutch armaments supplied to the Nguyen. For their part, the Nguyen expanded southwards again, absorbing the Khmer territories of the Mekong Delta.

Tay Son rebellion

In 1765 a rebellion erupted in the town of Tay Son near Qui Nhon. The Tay Son Rebels, as they soon became known, were led by the brothers Nguyen. In less than a decade they controlled the whole of central Vietnam. In 1783 they captured Saigon from the Nguyen Lords as well as the rest of the South, killing the reigning prince and his family. Nguyen Lu became king of the South, while Nguyen Nhac was crowned king of central Vietnam.

Continuing their conquests, the Tay Son Rebels overthrew the Trinh Lords in the North. Ever the opportunists, the Chinese moved in to take advantage of the power vacuum. In response, the third brother, Nguyen Hue, proclaimed himself Emperor Quang Trung. In 1789 Nguyen Hue's armed forces overwhelmingly defeated the Chinese army at Dong Da in another of the greatest hits of Vietnamese history.

In the South, Nguyen Anh, a rare survivor from the original Nguyen Lords – yes, know your Nguyens if you hope to understand Vietnamese history – gradually overcame the rebels. In 1802 Nguyen Anh proclaimed himself Emperor Gia Long, thus beginning the Nguyen dynasty. When he captured Hanoi, his victory was complete and, for the first time in two centuries, Vietnam was united, with Hué as its new capital city.

The last of the Nguyens

Emperor Gia Long returned to Confucian values in an effort to consolidate his precarious position. Conservative elements of the elite appreciated the familiar sense of order, which had evaporated in the dizzying atmosphere of reform stirred up by the Tay Son Rebels.

Gia Long's son, Emperor Minh Mang, worked to strengthen the state. He was profoundly hostile to Catholicism, which he saw as a threat to Confucian traditions, and extended this antipathy to all Western influences.

The early Nguyen emperors continued the expansionist policies of the preceding dynasties, pushing into Cambodia and westward into the mountains along a wide front. They seized huge areas of Lao territory and clashed with Thailand to pick apart the skeleton of the fractured Khmer empire.

The french takeover

France's military activity in Vietnam began in 1847, when the French Navy attacked Danang harbor in response to Emperor Thieu Tri's suppression of Catholic missionaries. Saigon was seized in early 1859 and, in 1862, Emperor Tu Duc signed a treaty that gave the French the three eastern provinces of Cochinchina. However, over the next four decades the French colonial venture in Indochina was carried out haphazardly and without any preconceived plan. It repeatedly faltered and, at times, only the reckless adventures of a few mavericks kept it going.

The next saga in French colonization began in 1872, when Jean Dupuis, a merchant seeking to supply salt and weapons to a Yunnanese general via the Red River, seized the Hanoi Citadel. Captain Francis Garnier, ostensibly dispatched to rein in Dupuis, instead took over where Dupuis left off and began a conquest of the North.

A few weeks after the death of Tu Duc in 1883, the French attacked Hué and imposed the Treaty of Protectorate on the imperial court.

There then began a tragi-comic struggle for royal succession that was notable for its palace coups, mysteriously dead emperors and heavy-handed French diplomacy.

The Indochinese Union proclaimed by the French in 1887 may have ended the existence of an independent Vietnamese state, but active resis-tance continued in various parts of the country for the duration of French rule. The expansionist era came to a close and the Vietnamese were forced to return territory seized from Cambodia and Laos.

The French colonial authorities carried out ambitious public works, such as the construction of the Saigon–Hanoi railway, the government taxed the peasants heavily to fund these activities, devastating the rural economy. Colonialism was supposed to be a profitable proposition, so operations became notorious for the low wages paid by the French and the poor treatment of Vietnamese workers. Out of the 45, 000 indentured workers at one Michelin rubber plantation, 12, 000 died of disease and malnutrition between 1917 and 1944. Shades of King Leopold's Congo.

Independence aspirations

Throughout the colonial period, a desire for independence simmered under the surface. Seething nationalist aspirations often erupted into open defiance of the French. This ranged from the publishing of patriotic periodicals to a dramatic attempt to poison the French garrison in Hanoi.

The imperial court in Hué, although quite corrupt, was a center of nationalist sentiment and the French orchestrated a game of musical thrones, as one emperor after another turned against their patronage. This comical caper culminated in the accession of Emperor Bao Dai in 1925, who was just 12 years old at the time and studying in France.

Ultimately, the most successful of the anticolonialists were the communists, who were able to tune into the frustrations and aspirations of the population – especially the peasants – and effectively channel their demands for fairer land distribution.

The story of Vietnamese communism, which in many ways is also the political biography of Ho Chi Minh, is complicated. Keeping it simple, the first Marxist grouping in Indochina was the Vietnam Revolutionary Youth League, founded by Ho Chi Minh in Canton, China, in 1925. This was succeeded in February 1930 by the Vietnamese Communist Party. In 1941 Ho formed the League for the Independence of Vietnam, much better known as the Viet Minh, which resisted the Japanese and carried out extensive political activities during WWII. Despite its nationalist programme, the Viet Minh was, from its inception, dominated by Ho's communists. But Ho was pragmatic, patriotic and populist and understood the need for national unity.

WWII breaks out

When France fell to Nazi Germany in 1940, the Indochinese government of Vichy France collaborators acquiesced to the presence of Japanese troops in Vietnam. For their own convenience the Japanese left the French administration in charge of the day-to-day running of the country. For a time, Vietnam was spared the ravages of Japanese occupation and things continued much as normal. However, as WWII drew to a close, Japanese rice requisitions, in combination with floods and breaches in the dikes, caused a horrific famine in which two million of North Vietnam's 10 million people starved to death. The only forces opposed to both the French and Japanese presence in Vietnam were the Viet Minh and Ho Chi Minh received assistance from the US government during this period. As events unfolded in Europe, the French and Japanese fell out and the Viet Minh saw its opportunity to strike.

A false dawn

By the spring of 1945 the Viet Minh controlled large parts of the country, particularly in the north. In mid-August, Ho Chi Minh formed the National Liberation Committee and called for a general uprising, later known as the August Revolution, to take advantage of the power vacuum. In central Vietnam, Bao Dai abdicated in favor of the new government, and in the South the Viet Minh soon held power in a shaky coalition with noncommunist groups. On 2 September 1945 Ho Chi Minh declared independence at a rally in Hanoi's Ba Dinh Square. Throughout this period, Ho wrote no fewer than eight letters to US president Harry Truman and the US State Department asking for US aid, but received no replies.

A footnote on the agenda of the Potsdam Conference of 1945 was the disarming of Japanese occupation forces in Vietnam. It was decided that the Chinese Kuomintang would accept the Japanese surrender north of the 16th Parallel and that the British would do the same to the south.

When the British arrived in Saigon, chaos reigned. The Japanese were defeated, the French were vulnerable, the Viet Minh was looking to assert itself, plus private militias were causing trouble. In order to help the Brits restore order, defeated Japanese troops were turned loose. Then 1400 armed French paratroopers were released from prison and, most likely looking for vengeance after Ho Chi Minh's declaration of independence, immediately went on a rampage around the city, breaking into the homes and shops of the Vietnamese and indiscriminately clubbing men, women and children. The Viet Minh responded by calling a general strike and by launching a guerrilla campaign against the French. On 24 September French general Jacques Philippe Leclerc arrived in Saigon, pompously declaring 'We have come to reclaim our inheritance'. The end of the war had brought liberation for France, but not, it seemed, for its colonies.

In the north, Chinese Kuomintang troops were fleeing the Chinese communists and pillaging their way southward towards Hanoi. Ho tried to placate them, but as the months of Chinese occupation dragged on, he decided 'better the devil you know' and accepted a temporary return of the French. For the Vietnamese, even the French colonizers were better than the Chinese. The French were to stay for five years in return for recognizing Vietnam as a free state within the French Union.

War with the French

The French had managed to regain control of Vietnam, at least in name. But when the French shelled Haiphong in November 1946, killing hundreds of civilians, the patience of the Viet Minh snapped. Only a few weeks later fighting broke out in Hanoi, marking the start of the Franco–Viet Minh War. Ho Chi Minh and his forces fled to the mountains, where they would remain for the next eight years.

In the face of determined Vietnamese nationalism, the French proved unable to reassert their control. Despite massive US aid (an effort to halt the communist domino effect throughout Asia) and the existence of significant indigenous anticommunist elements, it was an unwinnable war. As Ho said to the French at the time, 'You can kill 10 of my men for everyone I kill of yours, but even at those odds you will lose and I will win.'

After eight years of fighting, the Viet Minh controlled much of Vietnam and neighboring Laos. On 7 May 1954, after a 57-day siege, more than 10, 000 starving French troops surrendered to the Viet Minh at Dien Bien Phu. This was a catastrophic defeat that brought an end to the French colonial adventure in Indochina. The following day, the Geneva Conference opened to negotiate an end to the conflict. Resolutions included an exchange of prisoners; the temporary division of Vietnam into two zones at the Ben Hai River (near the 17th Parallel) until nationwide elections could be held; the free passage of people across the 17th Parallel for a period of 300 days; and the holding of nationwide elections on 20 July 1956. In the course of the Franco–Viet Minh War, more than 35, 000 French fighters had been killed and 48, 000 wounded; there are no exact numbers for Vietnamese casualties, but they were certainly far higher.

A separate South Vietnam

After the Geneva Accords were signed and sealed, the South was ruled by a government led by Ngo Dinh Diem, a fiercely anticommunist Catholic. His power base was significantly strengthened by 900, 000 refugees, many of them Catholics, who had fled the communist North during the 300-day free-passage period.

Nationwide elections were never held, as the Americans rightly feared that Ho Chi Minh would win with a massive majority. During the first few years of his rule, Diem consolidated power fairly effectively, defeating the Binh Xuyen crime syndicate and the private armies of the Hoa Hao and Cao Dai religious sects. During Diem's 1957 official visit to the USA, President Eisenhower called him the 'miracle man' of Asia. As time went on Diem became increasingly tyrannical in dealing with dissent. Running the government became a family affair.

In the early 1960s the South was rocked by anti-Diem unrest led by university students and Buddhist clergy, which included several highly publicized self-immolations by monks that shocked the world. The US decided Diem was a liability and threw its support behind a military coup. A group of young generals led the operation in November 1963. Diem was to go into exile, but the generals got over-excited and both Diem and his brother were killed. He was followed by a succession of military rulers who continued his erratic policies.

A new North Vietnam

The Geneva Accords allowed the leadership of the Democratic Republic of Vietnam to return to Hanoi and assert control of all territory north of the 17th Parallel. The new government immediately set out to eliminate those elements of the population that threatened its power. Tens of thousands of 'landlords', some with only tiny holdings, were denounced to 'security committees' by envious neighbors and arrested. Hasty 'trials' resulted in between 10, 000 and 15, 000 executions and the imprisonment of thousands more. In 1956, the party, faced with widespread rural unrest, recognized that things had got out of control and began a Campaign for the Rectification of Errors.

The North–South War

The campaign to 'liberate' the South began in 1959. The Ho Chi Minh Trail, which had been in existence for several years, was expanded. In April 1960 universal military conscription was implemented in the North. Eight months later, Hanoi announced the formation of the National Liberation Front (NLF), which came to be known, derogatorily, as the Viet Cong or the VC. Both are abbreviations for Viet Nam Cong San, which means Vietnamese communist. American soldiers nicknamed the VC 'Charlie'.

As the NLF launched its campaign, the Diem government rapidly lost control of the countryside. To stem the tide, the Strategic Hamlets Program was implemented in 1962, based on British tactics in Malaya. This involved forcibly moving peasants into fortified 'strategic hamlets' in order to deny the VC bases of support. This programme was abandoned with the death of Diem, but years later the VC admitted that it had caused them major problems.

And for the South it was no longer just a battle with the VC. In 1964 Hanoi began sending regular North Vietnamese Army (NVA) units down the Ho Chi Minh Trail. By early 1965 the Saigon government was on its last legs. Desertions from the Army of the Republic of Vietnam (ARVN), whose command was notorious for corruption and incompetence, had reached 2000 per month. The South was losing a district capital each week, yet in 10 years only one senior South Vietnamese army officer had been wounded. The army was getting ready to evacuate Hué and Danang, and the central highlands seemed about to fall. It was clearly time for the Americans to 'clean up the mess'.

Enter the cavalry

The Americans saw France's colonial war in Indochina as an important part of a worldwide struggle against communist expansion. Vietnam was the next domino and could not topple. In 1950, the US

Military Assistance Advisory Group (MAAG) rocked into Vietnam, ostensibly to instruct local troops in the efficiency of US firepower; there would be American soldiers on Vietnamese soil for the next 25 years, first as advisers, and then the main force. By 1954 US military aid to the French topped US$2 billion.

A decisive turning point in US strategy came with the August 1964 Gulf of Tonkin Incident. Two US destroyers, the Maddox and the Turner Joy, claimed to have come under 'unprovoked' attack while sailing off the North Vietnamese coast. Subsequent research indicates that there was plenty of provocation; the first attack took place while the Maddox was in North Vietnamese waters assisting a secret South Vietnamese commando raid and the second one never happened.

However, on US President Johnson's orders, 64 sorties rained bombs on the North – the first of thousands of such missions that would hit every single road and rail bridge in the country, as well as 4000 of North Vietnam's 5788 villages. Two US aircraft were lost and Lieutenant Everett Alvarez became the first American prisoner of war (POW) of the conflict; he would remain in captivity for eight years.

A few days later, an indignant (and misled) US Congress overwhelmingly passed the Tonkin Gulf Resolution, which gave the president the power to 'take all necessary measures' to 'repel any armed attack against the forces of the United States and to prevent further aggression'. Until its repeal in 1970, the resolution was treated by US presidents as carte blanche to do whatever they chose in Vietnam without any congressional control.

As the military situation of the Saigon government reached a new nadir, the first US combat troops splashed ashore at Danang in March 1965. By December 1965 there were 184, 300 US military personnel in Vietnam and 636 Americans had died. By December 1967 the figures had risen to 485, 600 US soldiers in country and 16, 021 dead. There were 1.3 million men fighting for the Saigon government, including the South Vietnamese and other allies.

By 1966 the buzz words in Washington were 'pacification', 'search and destroy' and 'free-fire zones'. Pacification involved developing a pro-government civilian infrastructure in each village, and providing the soldiers to guard it. To protect the villages from VC raids, mobile search-and-destroy units of soldiers moved around the country hunting VC guerrillas. In some cases, villagers were evacuated so the Americans could use heavy weaponry such as napalm and tanks in areas that were declared free-fire zones.

These strategies were only partially successful: US forces could control the countryside by day, while the VC usually controlled it by night. Even without heavy weapons, VC guerrillas continued to inflict heavy casualties in ambushes and by using mines and booby traps. Although free-fire zones were supposed to prevent civilian casualties, plenty of villagers were nevertheless shelled, bombed, strafed or napalmed to death – their surviving relatives soon signed up to join the VC.

The turning point

In January 1968 North Vietnamese troops launched a major attack at Khe Sanh in the Demilitarized Zone. This battle, the single largest of the war, was in part a massive diversion to draw attention away from the Tet Offensive.

The Tet Offensive marked a decisive turning point in the war. On the evening of 31 January, as the country celebrated the Lunar New Year, the VC launched a series of strikes in more than 100 cities and towns, including Saigon. As the TV cameras rolled, a VC commando team took over the courtyard of the US embassy in central Saigon.

US forces had long been itching to engage the VC in open battle and the Tet Offensive delivered. Although utterly surprised – a major failure of US military intelligence – the South Vietnamese and Americans immediately counterattacked with massive firepower, bombing and shelling heavily populated cities as they had the open jungle. The counterattack devastated the VC, but also traumatized the civilian population. In Ben Tre, a US officer bitterly remarked that they 'had to destroy the town in order to save it'.

The Tet Offensive killed about 1000 US soldiers and 2000 ARVN troops, but VC losses were more than 10 times higher, at around 32, 000 deaths. In addition, some 500 American and 10, 000 North Vietnamese troops had died at the battle of Khe Sanh the preceding week.

The VC may have lost the battle, but this was the critical turning point on the road to winning the war. The military had long been boasting that victory was just a matter for time. Watching the killing and chaos in Saigon beamed into their living rooms, many Americans stopped believing the hype. While US generals were proclaiming a great victory, public tolerance of the war and its casualties reached breaking point. For the VC the Tet Offensive ultimately proved a success: it made the cost of fighting the war unbearable for the Americans.

Simultaneously, stories began leaking out of Vietnam about atrocities and massacres carried out against unarmed Vietnamese civilians, including the infamous My Lai Massacre. This helped turn the tide and a coalition of the concerned emerged that threatened the establishment. Antiwar demonstrations rocked American university campuses and spilled onto the streets.

Nixon & his doctrine

Richard Nixon was elected president in part because of a promise that he had a 'secret plan' to end the war. The Nixon Doctrine, as it was called, was unveiled in July 1969 and it called on Asian nations to be more 'self-reliant' in defense matters. Nixon's strategy called for 'Vietnamization', which meant making the South Vietnamese fight the war without US troops. More recently, it's been dusted off for Iraq, but no-one has yet referred to it as the Bush Doctrine.

Even with the election of 'Tricky Dicky', the first half of 1969 saw yet greater escalation of the conflict. In April the number of US soldiers in Viet-nam reached an all-time high of 543, 400. While the fighting raged, Nixon's chief negotiator, Henry Kissinger, pursued peace talks in Paris with his North Vietnamese counterpart Le Duc Tho.

In 1969 the Americans began secretly bombing Cambodia in an attempt to flush out Vietnamese communist sanctuaries across the border. Given the choice between facing US troops and pushing deeper into Cambodia, they fled west. In 1970 US ground forces were sent into Cambodia to extricate ARVN units, whose combat ability was still unable to match the enemy's. The North Vietnamese moved deeper into Cambodian territory and together with their Khmer Rouge allies controlled half of the country by the summer of 1970, including the world-famous temples of Angkor.

This new escalation provoked yet more bitter antiwar protests. A peace demonstration at Kent State University in Ohio resulted in four protesters being shot dead by National Guard troops. The rise of organizations such as Vietnam Veterans Against the War demonstrated that it wasn't just 'cowardly students fearing military conscription' who wanted the USA out of Vietnam. It was clear that the war was tearing America apart.

In the spring of 1972 the North Vietnamese launched an offensive across the 17th Parallel; the USA responded with increased bombing of the North and by laying mines in North Vietnam's harbors. The 'Christmas bombing' of Haiphong and Hanoi at the end of 1972 was meant to wrest concessions from North Vietnam at the negotiating table. Eventually, the Paris Peace Accords were signed by the USA, North Vietnam, South Vietnam and the VC on 27 January 1973, which provided for a cease-fire, the total withdrawal of US combat forces and the release of 590 American POWs. The agreement failed to mention the 200, 000 North Vietnamese troops still in South Vietnam.

In total, 3.14 million Americans (including 7200 women) served in the US armed forces in Vietnam during the war. Officially, 58, 183 Americans were killed in action or are listed as missing in action (MIA). Pentagon figures indicate that by 1972, 3689 fixed-wing aircraft and 4857 helicopters had been lost and 15 million tonnes of ammunition had been expended. The direct cost of the war was officially put at US$165 billion, though its real cost to the economy was double that or more.

By the end of 1973, 223, 748 South Vietnamese soldiers had been killed in action; North Vietnamese and VC fatalities have been estimated at one million. Approximately four million civilians (or 10% of the Vietnamese population) were injured or killed during the war, many of them as a direct result of US bombing in the North. At least 300, 000 Vietnamese and 2200 Americans are still listed as MIA or 'Missing in Action'. US teams continue to search Vietnam, Laos and Cambodia for the remains of their fallen comrades. In more recent years, the Vietnamese have been searching for their own MIAs in Cambodia and Laos. Individual family members often use mediums to try and locate the remains of their loved ones.

Other foreign involvement

Australia, New Zealand, South Korea, the Philippines and Thailand also sent military personnel to South Vietnam as part of what the Americans called the 'Free World Military Forces', whose purpose was to help internationalize the American war effort and thus confer upon it some legitimacy. Sound familiar?

Australia's participation in the conflict constituted the most significant commitment of its military forces since WWII. There were 46, 852 Australian military personnel that served in the war; the Australian casualties totaled 496 dead and 2398 wounded.

Most of New Zealand's contingent, which numbered 548 at its high point in 1968, operated as an integral part of the Australian Task Force, which was stationed near Baria, just north of Vung Tau.

The fall of The South

All US military personnel departed Vietnam in 1973, leaving behind a small contingent of technicians and CIA agents. The bombing of North Vietnam ceased and the US POWs were released. Still the war raged on, only now the South Vietnamese were fighting alone.

In January 1975 the North Vietnamese launched a massive ground attack across the 17th Parallel using tanks and heavy artillery. The invasion provoked panic in the South Vietnamese army, which had always depended on the Americans. In March, the NVA occupied a strategic section of the central highlands at Buon Ma Thuot. South Vietnam's president, Nguyen Van Thieu, decided on a strategy of tactical withdrawal to more defensible positions. This proved to be a spectacular military blunder.

Whole brigades of ARVN soldiers disintegrated and fled southward, joining hundreds of thousands of civilians clogging Hwy 1. City after city – Hué, Danang, Quy Nhon, Nha Trang – were simply abandoned with hardly a shot fired. The ARVN troops were fleeing so quickly that the North Vietnamese army could barely keep up.

Nguyen Van Thieu, in power since 1967, resigned on 21 April 1975 and fled the country, allegedly carting off millions of dollars in ill-gotten wealth. The North Vietnamese pushed on to Saigon and on the morning of 30 April 1975 their tanks smashed through the gates of Saigon's Independence Palace (now called Reunification Palace). General Duong Van Minh, president for just 42 hours, formally surrendered, marking the end of the war.

Just a few hours before the surrender, the last Americans were evacuated by helicopter from the US embassy roof to ships stationed just offshore. Iconic images of US Marines booting Vietnamese people off their helicopters were beamed around the world. And so more than a quarter of a century of American military involvement came to a close. Throughout the entire conflict, the USA never actually declared war on North Vietnam.

The Americans weren't the only ones who left. As the South collapsed, 135, 000 Vietnamese also fled the country; in the next five years, at least half a million of their compatriots would do the same. Those who left by sea would become known to the world as 'boat people'. These refugees risked everything to undertake perilous journeys on the South China Sea. Pirates raped and pillaged, storms raged, but eventually these hardy souls found a new life in places as diverse as Australia and France.

Reunification of Vietnam

On the first day of their victory, the communists changed Saigon's name to Ho Chi Minh City (HCMC). This was just the first of many changes.

The sudden success of the 1975 North Vietnamese offensive surprised the North almost as much as it did the South. Consequently, Hanoi had no specific plans to deal with the reintegration of the North and South, which had totally different social and economic systems.

The North was faced with the legacy of a cruel and protracted war that had literally fractured the country. There was bitterness on both sides, and a mind-boggling array of problems. Damage from the fighting extended from unmarked minefields to war-focused, dysfunctional economies; from a chemically poisoned countryside to a population who had been physically or mentally battered. Peace may have arrived, but in many ways the war was far from over.

Until the formal reunification of Vietnam in July 1976, the South was ruled by the Provisional Revolutionary Government. The Communist Party did not trust the Southern urban intelligentsia, so large numbers of Northern cadres were sent southward to manage the transition. This fueled resentment among Southerners who had worked against the Thieu government and then, after its overthrow, found themselves frozen out.

The party decided on a rapid transition to socialism in the South, but it proved disastrous for the economy. Reunification was accompanied by widespread political repression. Despite repeated promises to the contrary, hundreds of thousands of people who had ties to the previous regime had their property confiscated and were rounded up and imprisoned without trial in forced-labor camps, euphemistically known as re-education camps. Tens of thousands of businesspeople, intellectuals, artists, journalists, writers, union leaders and religious leaders – some of whom had opposed both Thieu and the war – were held in horrendous conditions.

Contrary to its economic policy, Vietnam sought some sort of rapprochement with the USA and by 1978 Washington was close to establishing relations with Hanoi. But the China card was ultimately played: Vietnam was sacrificed for the prize of US relations with Beijing and Hanoi was pushed into the arms of the Soviet Union, on whom it was to rely for the next decade.

Relations with China to the north and its Khmer Rouge allies to the west were rapidly deteriorating and war-weary Vietnam seemed beset by enemies. An anti-capitalist campaign was launched in March 1978, seizing private property and businesses. Most of the victims were ethnic Chinese – hundreds of thousands soon became refugees or 'boat people', and relations with China soured further.

Meanwhile, repeated attacks on Vietnamese border villages by the Khmer Rouge forced Vietnam to respond. Vietnamese forces entered Cambodia on Christmas Day 1978. They succeeded in driving the Khmer Rouge from power on 7th January 1979 and set up a pro-Hanoi regime in Phnom Penh. China viewed the attack on the Khmer Rouge as a serious provocation. In February 1979 Chinese forces invaded Vietnam and fought a brief, 17-day war before withdrawing.

Liberation of Cambodia from the Khmer Rouge soon turned to occupation and a long civil war. The command economy was strangling the commercial instincts of Vietnamese rice farmers. Today, the world's leading rice exporter, by the early 1980s Vietnam was a rice importer. War and revolution had brought the country to its knees and a radical change in direction was required.

Opening the door

In 1985 President Mikhael Gorbachev came to power in the Soviet Union. Glasnost (openness) and perestroika (restructuring) were in, radical revolutionaries were out. Vietnam followed suit in 1986 by choosing reform-minded Nguyen Van Linh to lead the Vietnamese Communist Party. Doi moi (economic reform) was experimented with in Cambodia and introduced to Vietnam. As the USSR scaled back its commitments to the communist world, the far-flung outposts were the first to feel the pinch. The Vietnamese decided to unilaterally withdraw from Cambodia in 1989, as they could no longer afford the occupation. The party in Vietnam was on its own and needed to reform to survive.

However, dramatic changes in Eastern Europe in 1989 and the collapse of the Soviet Union in 1991 were not viewed with favor in Hanoi. The party denounced the participation of noncommunists in Eastern Bloc governments, calling the democratic revolutions 'a counterattack from imperialist circles' against socialism. Politically things were moving at a glacial pace, but economically the Vietnamese decided to embrace the market. It has taken time, but capitalism has taken root and it is unlikely Ho Chi Minh would recognize the dynamic Vietnam of today.

Vietnam today

Relations with Vietnam's old nemesis, the USA, have improved in recent years. In early 1994 the USA finally lifted its economic embargo, which had been in place since the 1960s. Full diplomatic relations with the USA have been restored and Bill Clinton, who didn't fight in the war (and didn't inhale!), became the first US president to visit northern Vietnam in 2000. George W Bush followed suit in 2006, as Vietnam was welcomed into the World Trade Organization (WTO).

Relations have also improved with the historic enemy China. Vietnam is still overshadowed by its northern neighbor and China still secretly thinks of Vietnam as a renegade province. But Vietnam's economic boom has caught Beijing's attention and it sees northern Vietnam as the fastest route from Yunnan and Sichuan to the South China Sea. Cooperation towards the future is more important than the conflict of the past.

Vietnam is an active member of Asean, an organization originally established as a bulwark against communism, and this is all adding up to a rosy economic picture. Vietnam's economy is growing at more than 8% a year and tourists just can't get enough of the place. The future is bright, but ultimate success depends on how well the Vietnamese can follow the Chinese road to development: economic liberalization without political liberalization. With only two million paid-up members of the Communist Party and 80 million Vietnamese, it is a road they must tread carefully.

Typical Costs

Accommodation

Hostels start at 130,000 VND per night. Private rooms average about 390,000 VND for a double room. In the past hostels were pretty scarce, though recently, hostels have started popping up all over the country to accommodate budget travelers. "Homestays" are often popular budget option, too.

Food

By eating at street stalls and markets you can get a bowl of pho or a rice dish for 20,000 VND. Most sit down restaurants are also inexpensive at around 40,000–90,000 VND. The fancier (and more touristy) the restaurant, the more expensive. A liter of water at a convenience store is about 15,000 VND, while a beer or soda at a restaurant is about 20,000-35,000 VND.

Transportation

Bus travel is very cheap in Vietnam. For example, the public bus around Ho Chi Minh City will cost a maximum of 3,500 VND. The train is also another inexpensive way to travel with the 791km long train journey from Da Nang to Hanoi costing 750,000 VND. Overnight buses (aside from saving on a night's accommodation) are only about 100,000-500,000 VND and can take you to lots of cities in Vietnam. There are extremely low-cost airlines that can hop you around the country quickly for as little as 400,000 VND.

Activities

Many of Vietnam's attractions are based around its natural beauty and as such, cost very little. For organized excursions such as touring the Cu Chi Tunnels you can expect to pay between 100,000–200,000 VND. Ha long Bay tours from Hanoi start at 650,000 VND for two-day trips and increase exponentially from there. Half-day cooking classes and bicycle tours are heavily targeted at tourists, so they cost a bit more, and start at about 300,000 VND.

Money Saving Tips

Eat street food

The food is usually excellent, really cheap and you can watch it being cooked in front of you. Stick to the local food and you'll save money. The street-side pho, bread, meat sandwiches (called bahn mi), donuts, and bananas are your best deals all of which can be found around 20,000 VND on the streets.

Late-night travel

If traveling long journeys, try to take the late night "sleeper" buses or trains as this will save you the cost of a night's accommodation. Depending on the company, you may even have a chance to comfortably lie flat as you ride through the dark countryside to your next destination.

Take the tourist bus

It is actually cheaper to take the tourist bus around the country than taking local transportation because of the "tourist" price you get at the bus station.

Don't be afraid of taxis

Metered taxis in this country are affordable. If you are moving around town at night, this is a good, safe, cheap option (especially if you're splitting the cost with a few others). A 30-minute ride will set you back around 130,000 VND. The best taxi companies are Mai Linh and Vinasun.

Fly for cheap

Vietnam's low-cost airlines: VietJet and FlyVietnam are extremely inexpensive and adding luggage to your flight can cost as little s 120,000 VND. This is a great option for people with limited time to explore different regions of Vietnam.

Bargain hard

Tourists tend to be charged more than locals for everything from cycles (a three-wheel bicycle taxi) to clothes to street food. Bargain harder than you would ordinarily, and don't underestimate the value of walking away.

Skip the SIM Card

Vietnam is highly connected to Wi-Fi. You can hook into Wi-Fi in just about every hotel, shop, restaurant, and convenience store for free! Unless you need to have connectivity during long bus rides or rural areas, I'd forgo the SIM card and take a break from connectivity.

Ask your hostel staff

Before you leave the hostel, ask them to estimate how much what you want to do should cost. How much should a ride to the museum cost? How much should I pay to have a gown like this made? They will be able to give you bargaining guidelines.

Stay a while

You'll hear tales from many backpackers who have been to many different Vietnamese regions on a very short trip. A good way to save money and savor the experience is to slow down. Divide your time between a few spots and enjoy.

Factor in visa fees

Visiting Vietnam comes with a much higher visa fees than the surrounding Southeast Asian countries. Look up the visa requirements and fees before you arrive. Better to be safe than sorry!

Top Things to See and Do in Vietnam

Admire the pagodas

Vietnam's most distinctive architecture can be seen in the pagodas, which can be found all over the country. They are known for their beautifully intricate carvings. Pagodas are used as shrines and temples and are treasured by the Vietnamese people.

Wander around Hanoi

Vietnam's capital, Hanoi handsomely combines French colonialism with Eastern influences. Enjoy an afternoon exploring the narrow streets of the Old Quarter or visit the countless temples and galleries dotted around this bustling city. Don't miss the History Museum which showcases artifacts from Vietnam's colorful history and the Ho Chi Minh City Mausoleum. Hanoi is also a good base for doing multi-day tours to Halong Bay, Hua Lu and Tam Coc.

Relax or find adventure in Dalat

Dalat is nestled in the hills of the Central Highlands and is popular with tourists who want to relax in the mountain air, so people flock here for serenity. Others go to Dalat to participate in a host of adventure sports that happen within a naturally beautiful backdrop. The hills around Dalat are filled with traditional tribal villages, which you can tour, but there is plenty to do within the city itself too. Visit the imaginatively titled palaces: Palace I, Palace II and Palace III.

Tour the Mekong Delta

The delta is a 60,000km long web of interconnected waterways, which span across three Vietnamese provinces. The area is filled with small craft villages, Khmer Pagodas, mangroves, orchards and the trademark floating markets. The best way to experience Delta life is to go on one of the many boat or bike tours. Spend a few days exploring the stunning region.

Crawl through the Cu Chi Tunnels

Crawl through the extensive network of nearly 500 km of tunnels utilized by the Viet Cong in the war with the USA in the 1960s. Tours involve a description of the tunnels, after which tourists are allowed to crawl about the maze and fire AK47s at shooting targets. It's a sobering experience and not one meant for anyone claustrophobic. However, if you want a better understand the terror of the Vietnam War, this is a must-visit. Enter for about 100,000 VND.

Visit Cuc Phuong National Park

About 120km southwest of Hanoi lies Vietnam's first National Park, Cuc Phuong. Covering 222 sq. km, this place is home to over 2,000 species of trees and some truly rare wildlife including the Clouded Leopard, Delacour's Langur and Owston's Civet. It was my favorite park in all of Vietnam and the only place I didn't find hordes of tourists. The entrance fee is 40,000 VND.

Hang out in Hoi An

Hoi An is one of the most popular destinations for tourists traveling to the country. The place is packed with historical homes and buildings and quaint cafes. It's small and great for walking, buying suits (they have a huge fashion and tailor market), eating, nearby beaches, and relaxing by the river. It was easily my favorite place in Vietnam. It's not unusual to find backpackers using Noi An as a resting ground while they recharge from constant traveling. This is a relaxing quality to it that makes staying for a while very attractive.

Explore Ho Chi Minh City

Also known as Saigon, Ho Chi Minh City is Vietnam's largest city and is definitely worth exploring. Like most cities in Vietnam, you'll be met with the roar of motorbikes speeding through colonial streets. Ben Thanh market is a must-see for amazing food and there is a great buzz of activity within the place. If flying into the SGN airport, it's worth spending a day or two exploring the city. I recommend spending the night at The Common Room Project for a great hostel experience.

Hike in Halong Bay

More than 3,000 islands sit within the emerald green waters of Halong Bay, one of the country's most popular tourist destinations. Cat Ba Island has great for hiking and many tourists find themselves taking one of the cave tours. Tours here usually leave from Hanoi and last 3 or 5 days. Try to find a good operator as many oversell or lie about what their boats look like (ask for advice from your hotel staff or travelers who have just returned for the trip).

Get active in Mui Ne

Despite being a fishing village, Mui Ne has got a significant tourism scene, due to its popularity as a wind- and kite-surfing destination, and the rolling sand dunes that lie nearby.

See My Son

My Son is a set of Hindu ruins in Vietnam which date back to the Cham Empire. The Champas ruled over Central Vietnam from the 3rd to the 19th century. The temples here are of incredible historical importance, but they have been largely reclaimed by the surrounding jungle, and have fallen into a great state of disrepair. Don't come here expecting something as marvelously preserved as Borobudur or Angkor Wat. Entrance fee is 100,000 VND for foreigners.

Visit the caves in Phong Nha-Ke Bang

Hang Son Doong is reputed to be the world's largest cave, and is located in Phong Nha-Ke Bang National Park. It was discovered by a local in 1990, and "rediscovered" by a British caving team in 2009. You can arrange trips to see this stunning cave. You'll be blown away by its beauty.

Dive in Nha Trang

This area is full of seaside resorts, and has a distinct urban feel. However, the beautiful sand and clear water make it a main spot for scuba diving in Vietnam.

Check out the rice terraces

Outside of connections to the Vietnam War, the stereotypical image of Vietnam is of the many rice paddies. You can find these in the Muong Hoa Valley. If you've never visited rice terraces, you should make a point to see them in Vietnam. Visit them to learn about rice production and take stunning photographs of the unbelievable Vietnamese countryside.

6 tips for first-time travelers to Vietnam

1. Keep smiling

Despite the grumbles of many visitors, Vietnamese people are mostly just as friendly as their Southeast Asian counterparts. However, unlike in Thailand, Cambodia and Laos - where local residents are genuinely curious about who you are and where you've come from - Vietnamese people tend to ignore lost-looking foreigners unless you actually ask for help. But be assured that if you ask a local a question with a smile, you'll almost certainly have it answered and the smile returned.

2. Be wary of taxi scams

For many, motorcycle taxis are the only way to truly see the thronging streets of Hanoi and Ho Chi Minh. However, although unlikely, scams can happen and your best protection is a decent knowledge of where you are going and points along the way. If you think you're going the wrong way, simply tell your driver to pull over and flag down a new bike - those that stop should at least know the English names of the main tourist sights. Also, organize for a hotel pick-up from the airport - scam taxis are rife and, as my quickly lightened wallet can attest, far more expensive and stressful than the $5 you supposedly could save.

3. Know your night buses

Overnight buses are a great way to cover long distances and save on accommodation costs, but make sure you book a top bunk as far as possible from the loo (normally situated near the back). Not to put too fine a point on it, a lot of buses don't have working bathrooms and the further back you are, the worse the smell gets. Also, unless you have an iron bladder, don't drink more than absolutely necessary, as rest stops seem to be purely at the whim of the driver and are skipped completely if the bus is running late. On one seven-hour bus trip - that ended up being a 16-hour voyage - I was very glad to have followed this tip. Not all of the other passengers had done so - enough said!

4. Avoid nightlife trouble

Vietnam has possibly the cheapest beer in the world but it pays not to overdo it. In Hanoi there is an official curfew on bars and nightclubs, which the police may turn up and enforce unless the owner has paid a suitable 'fee'. Hiding in the dark as the club pretends to be closed while a police car drives by can be amusing, but it sucks when half your group gets thrown out by the cops and can't get back in. Meanwhile, Nha Trang leaves a sorry trail of wallet-lightened backpackers who experienced the not-uncommon misfortune of running into pickpocketing prostitutes - and attendant gangs - on their way home after a night out.

5. Motorcycle safely

Clarkson may have done it, but he had a whole production crew and still ended up with a couple of broken ribs. Vietnam is not the place to learn to ride a motorbike. I have rarely been as scared as the moment I had to cross a traffic-light-free four-lane junction where scooters dodged each other by mere inches. The roads are truly terrifying and unfortunately the stories of tourists killed attempting a two-wheeled adventure are all too based in fact.

If you're determined to get the thrill of a bike, it's worth looking into the Dalat Easy Rider (dalat-easyrider.com) where an experienced Vietnamese rider will take care of the driving so you can sit back and enjoy the scenery.

6. Be bold

Most important of all: don't be scared. Vietnam can seem intimidating and overwhelming at first, but keep a sense of humor and everything will work out fine. Just like the streets of Hanoi, where to cross the road you have to wade out into moving traffic whispering prayers to any and every god that you won't get hit, the worst thing you can do is freeze. Keep moving at a steady pace and the bedlam will slowly envelop and glide around you - until magically you are right where you wanted to be without a single scratch!

Where to go

The "Hanoi or bust" attitude, prompting new arrivals to doggedly labor between the country's two major cities, no matter how limited their time, blights many a trip to Vietnam. If you want to travel the length of the country at some leisure, see something of the highlands and the deltas and allow for a few rest days, you'll really need a month. With only two weeks at your disposal, the choice is either to hopscotch up the coast calling at only the most mainstream destinations or, perhaps better, to concentrate on one region and enjoy it at your own pace. However, if you do want to see both north and south in a fortnight, internal flights can speed up an itinerary substantially, and aren't too expensive.

For the majority of visitors, Ho Chi Minh City provides a head-spinning introduction to Vietnam. Set beside the broad swell of the Saigon River, the southern capital is rapidly being transformed into a Southeast Asian mover and shaker to compete with the best of them. The city's breakneck pace of life translates into a stew of bizarre characters and unlikely sights and sounds, and ensures that almost all who come here quickly fall for its singular charm. Furious commerce carries on cheek-by-jowl with age-old traditions; grandly indulgent colonial edifices peek out from under the shadows of looming office blocks and hotels; and cyclo drivers battle it out with late-model Japanese taxis in the chaotic boulevards.

Few tourists pass up the opportunity to take a day-trip out of the city to Tay Ninh, the nerve center of the indigenous Cao Dai religion. The jury is still out on whether the Cao Dai Holy See constitutes high art or dog's dinner, but either way it's one of Vietnam's most arresting sights, and is normally twinned with a stop-off at the Cu Chi tunnels, where Vietnamese villagers dug themselves a warren stretching over two hundred kilometers, out of reach of US bombing.

Another destination easily reached from Ho Chi Minh City is the Mekong Delta, where one of the world's truly mighty rivers finally offloads into the South China Sea; its skein of brim-full tributaries and waterways has endowed the delta with a lush quilt of rice paddies and abundant orchards. You won't want to depart the delta without spending a day or more messing about on the water and visiting a floating market, which is easily arranged at Cai Be and Can Tho.

Da Lat, the gateway to the central highlands, is chalk to Ho Chi Minh City's cheese. Life passes by at a rather more dignified pace at an altitude of 1500m, and the fresh breezes that fan this oddly quaint hillside settlement provide the best air conditioning in Vietnam. Minority peoples inhabit the countryside around Da Lat, but to visit some really full-on montagnard villages you'll need to push north to the modest towns of Buon Ma Thuot, Pleiku and Kon Tum, which are surrounded by E De, Jarai and Bahnar communities. Opt for Kon Tum, and you'll be able to visit minority villages independently or join treks that include river-rafting.

Northeast of Ho Chi Minh City, Highway 1, the country's jugular, carries the lion's share of traffic up to Hanoi and the north, though the recently completed Ho Chi Minh Highway offers drivers a tempting alternative route. For many people, the first stop along Highway 1 is at the delightful beach and sand dunes of Mui Ne, fast becoming one of the country's top coastal resorts. Further north, Nha Trang is another beach resort that also boasts a lively nightlife, and the tirelessly touted boat trips around the city's outlying islands are a must. North of Nha Trang, near Quang Ngai, Son My village attained global notoriety when a company of American soldiers massacred some five hundred Vietnamese, including many women and children; unspeakable horrors continue to haunt the village's unnervingly idyllic rural setting.

Once a bustling seaport, the diminutive town of Hoi An perches beside an indolent backwater, its narrow streets of wooden-fronted shop houses and weathered roofs making it an enticing destination. Inland, the war-battered ruins of My Son, the greatest of the Cham temple sites, lie moldering in a steamy, forest-filled valley. Da Nang, just up the coast, lacks Hoi An's charm, but good transport links make it a convenient base for the area. From Da Nang a corkscrew ride over clifftop Hai Van Pass, or a straight run through the new 6km-long tunnel, brings you to the aristocratic city of Hué, where the Nguyen emperors established their capital in the nineteenth century on the banks of the languid Perfume River. The temples and palaces of this highly cultured city still testify to past splendors, while its Imperial mausoleums are masterpieces of architectural refinement, slumbering among pine-shrouded hills.

Only a hundred kilometers north of Hué, the tone changes as war-sites litter the Demilitarized Zone (DMZ), which cleaved the country in two from 1954 to 1975. More than three decades of peace have done much to heal the scars, but the monuments that pepper these windswept hills bear eloquent witness to a generation that lost their lives in the tragic struggle. The DMZ is most easily tackled as a day-trip from Hué, after which most people hop straight up to Hanoi. And there's little to detain you on the northward trek, save the glittering limestone caverns of Phong Nha, the entrance to a massive underground river system tunneling under the Truong Son Mountains, which includes Son Doong, discovered in 2009 and now thought to be the largest cave in the world. Then, on the very fringes of the northern Red River Delta, lie the ancient incense-steeped temples of Hoa Lu and, nearby, the mystical landscapes of Tam Coc and Van Long, where paddy fields lap at the feet of limestone hummocks.

Anchored firmly in the Red River Delta, Hanoi has served as Vietnam's capital for over a thousand years. It's a rapidly-growing, decidedly proud city, a place of pagodas and dynastic temples, tamarisk-edged lakes and elegant boulevards of French-era villas, of national monuments and stately government edifices. But Hanoi is also being swept along on a tide of change as Vietnam forges its own shiny, high-rise capital, throwing up new office blocks, hotels and restaurants.

From Hanoi most visitors strike out east to where northern Vietnam's premier natural attraction, Ha Long Bay, provides the perfect antidote to such urban exuberance, rewarding the traveler with a leisurely day or two drifting among the thousands of whimsically sculpted islands anchored in its aquamarine waters. Ha Long City, on the northern coast, is the most popular embarkation point for Ha Long Bay, but a more appealing gateway is mountainous Cat Ba Island, which defines the bay's southwestern limits. The route to Cat Ba passes via the north's major port city, Hai Phong, an unspectacular but genial place with an attractive core of faded colonial facades.

To the north and west of Hanoi mountain ranges rear up out of the Red River Delta. Vietnam's northern provinces aren't the easiest to get around, but these wild uplands are home to a patchwork of ethnic minorities and the country's most dramatic mountain landscapes. The bustling market town of Sa Pa, set in a spectacular location close to the Chinese border in the far northwest, makes a good base for exploring nearby minority villages, though a building boom has taken some of the shine off its laidback vibe. Southwest of Hanoi, the stilt house-filled valley of Mai Chau offers an opportunity to stay in a minority village. Though few people venture further inland, backroads heading upcountry link isolated outposts and give access to the Northwest's only specific sight, where the French colonial dream expired in the dead-end valley of Dien Bien Phu. East of the Red River Valley lies an even less-frequented region, whose prime attraction is its varied scenery, from the vertigo-inducing valleys of the Dong Van Karst Plateau Geopark to the limestone crags and multi-layered rainforest of Ba Be National Park, and the remote valleys around Cao Bang, farmed by communities still practicing their traditional ways of life.

When to go

When deciding the best time to visit Vietnam, consider the country's tropical monsoon climate, dominated by the south or southwesterly monsoon from May to September and the northeast monsoon from October to April. The southern summer monsoon brings rain to the two deltas and west-facing slopes, while the cold winter monsoon picks up moisture over the Gulf of Tonkin and dumps it along the central coast and the eastern edge of the central highlands. Within this basic pattern there are marked differences according to altitude and latitude; temperatures in the south remain equable all year round, while the north experiences distinct seasonal variations.

In southern Vietnam the dry season lasts from December to late April or May, and the rains from May through to November. Since most rain falls in brief afternoon downpours, this need not be off-putting, though flooding at this time of year can cause problems in the Mekong Delta. Daytime temperatures in the region rarely drop below 20°C, occasionally hitting 40°C during the hottest months (March, April and May). The climate of the central highlands generally follows the same pattern, though temperatures are cooler, especially at night. Again, the monsoon rains of May to October can make transport more complicated, sometimes washing out roads and cutting off remoter villages.

Along the central coast the rainfall pattern reverses under the influence of the northeast monsoon. Around Nha Trang the wet season starts with a flourish in November and continues through December. Further north, around Hué and Da Nang, the rains last a bit longer, from September to February, so it pays to visit these two cities in the spring (Feb–May). Temperatures reach their maximum (often in the upper 30s) from June to August, when it's pleasant to escape into the hills. The northern stretches of this coastal region experience a more extreme climate, with a shorter rainy season (peaking in Sept and Oct) and a hot dry summer. The coast of central Vietnam is the zone most likely to be hit by typhoons, bringing torrential rain and hurricane-force winds. Though notoriously difficult to predict, in general the typhoon season lasts from August to November.

Northern Vietnam is generally warm and sunny from October to December, after which cold winter weather sets in, accompanied by fine persistent mists which can last for several days. Temperatures begin to rise again in March, building to summer maximums that occasionally reach 40°C between May and August, though average temperatures in Hanoi hover around a more reasonable 30°C. However, summer is also the rainy season, when heavy downpours render the low-lying delta area almost unbearably hot and sticky, and flooding is a regular hazard. The northern mountains share the same basic regime, though temperatures are considerably cooler and higher regions see ground frosts, or even a rare snowfall, during the winter (Dec–Feb).

With such a complicated weather picture, there's no one particular season to recommend as the best time for visiting Vietnam. Overall, autumn (Sept–Dec) and spring (March and April) are probably the most favorable seasons if you're covering the whole country.

Getting to Vietnam

The number of direct flights to Vietnam's three main international airports – Ho Chi Minh City, Hanoi and Da Nang, in order of importance – have increased steadily in recent years. However, the majority of visitors take the cheaper option of an indirect flight routed through Bangkok, Singapore or Hong Kong; a stay in one of these cities can be factored into your schedule, often at no extra cost. You may well save even more by taking a bargain–basement flight to Bangkok, Kuala Lumpur or Singapore, and a separate ticket through one of the region's low–cost carriers, such as Jetstar, Tiger Airways and Air Asia, for the Vietnam leg.

Airlines that fly in and out of both Hanoi and Ho Chi Minh City normally sell you an open-jaw ticket, which allows you to fly into one city and out of the other, leaving you to travel up or down the country under your own steam.

Airfares always depend on the season, with the highest generally being July to August, during the Christmas and New Year holidays and around Tet, the Vietnamese New Year; fares drop during the "shoulder" season – September to mid-December – and you'll get the best prices during the low season, January to June.

You can often cut costs by going through a specialist flight agent – either a consolidator, who buys up blocks of tickets from the airlines and sells them at a discount, or a discount agent, who in addition to dealing with discounted flights may also offer special student and youth fares and a range of other travel-related services such as travel insurance, rail passes, car rentals, tours and the like.

Combining Vietnam with other Southeast Asian countries is becoming increasingly popular – and a lot cheaper and easier – thanks to some good-value regional air deals. Jetstar (jetstar.com), for example, flies from Singapore to Ho Chi Minh City (from $50 one-way), while Tiger Airways (tigerairways.com) flies from Singapore to Hanoi (from $70 one-way) and Ho Chi Minh City (from $50 one-way). Air Asia (airasia.com) offers daily services from Bangkok and Kuala Lumpur to both Hanoi and Ho Chi Minh City, with fares starting at $50 one-way to Ho Chi Minh City, and a little more to Hanoi. As with all discount airlines, prices depend on availability, so the earlier you book the better, though you may also find last-minute promotional fares, seat giveaways and so forth at less busy times of the year.

From the UK and Ireland

There are as yet no non-stop flights to Vietnam from the UK or Ireland (believed to be starting with Vietnam Airlines in December 2011). Instead, most people fly with a Southeast Asian carrier such as Singapore Airlines (singaporeair.com), Thai Airways (thaiairways.com), Malaysia Airlines (malaysiaairlines.com) or Cathay Pacific (cathaypacific.com) from London via the airline's home city. In recent years the big Middle Eastern airlines, Qatar (qatarairways.com) and Emirates (emirates.com), have also offered very competitive prices. Scheduled low-season fares from London start at around £450, rising to £600 or more at peak periods.

A good place to look for the best deals is the travel sections of the weekend newspapers and in regional listings magazines. Students and under-26s can often get discounts through specialist agents such as STA (sta.com) or USIT in Ireland (usit.ie). Whoever you buy your ticket through, check that the agency belongs to the travel industry bodies ABTA or IATA, so that you'll be covered if the agent goes bust before you get your ticket.

From the USA and Canada

In 2004 United Airlines (united.com) became the first American carrier to resume direct flights to Vietnam since 1975. The airline operates a daily service from San Francisco to Ho Chi Minh City via Hong Kong; standard return fares start at around $1100. As yet, no other American or Canadian carriers offer direct services, which means you'll either have to get a flight to San Francisco or catch one of the many flights to a regional hub, such as Bangkok, Singapore or Hong Kong, and continue on from there. Scheduled flights start at around $1400 from New York, $1200 from Los Angeles, CAN$2000 from Vancouver and CAN$2500 from Toronto.

Note that some routings require an overnight stay in another city such as Bangkok, Taipei, Hong Kong or Seoul, and often a hotel room will be included in your fare – ask the airline and shop around since travel agents' policies on this vary. Even when an overnight stay is not required, going to Vietnam can be a great excuse for a stopover: most airlines will allow you one free stopover in either direction.

From Australia and New Zealand

A reasonable range of flights connects Australia and New Zealand with Vietnam, with Qantas (qantas.com), Vietnam Airlines (vietnamairlines.com) and Jetstar offering direct services from Australia. The alternative is to fly to another Asian gateway, such as Bangkok, Kuala Lumpur, Singapore or Hong Kong, and then either get connecting flights or travel overland to Hanoi or Ho Chi Minh City.

By far the cheapest flight from Australia is the daily Jetstar service to Ho Chi Minh City from Sydney (AUS$390 one-way) via Darwin (AUS$250 one-way). Both Vietnam Airlines and Qantas operate direct flights to Ho Chi Minh City from Melbourne and Sydney; low-season scheduled fares start at around AUS$1100 with Vietnam Airlines, with Qantas often a little cheaper. If you want to stop off on the way, there are good deals to Hanoi and Ho Chi Minh City with Malaysia Airlines via Kuala Lumpur, Singapore Airlines via Singapore, and Thai Airways via Bangkok, all costing around AUS$1100 to AUS$1500. Cheaper still are the fares offered by Tiger Airways, a discount airline operating daily flights between Perth and Singapore: one-way fares sometimes dip below AUS$200. From Singapore you can get an onward flight to Hanoi (from around AUS$100 one-way) or Ho Chi Minh City (from around AUS$55 one-way).

From New Zealand, low-season fares with Malaysia Airlines, Thai, Qantas and Singapore Airlines are all around NZ$1500 to NZ$2200, with a change of plane in the carrier's home airport.

From neighboring countries

It's increasingly popular to enter Vietnam overland from China, Laos or Cambodia, an option that means you can see more of the region than you would if you simply jetted in. However, it must be said that regional air connections are becoming better and better – you can fly from many cities in Southern China, from Phnom Penh or Siem Reap with Cambodia Angkor Air (bookable through codeshare partner Vietnam Airlines), or from Vientiane with Vietnam Airlines or Lao Airlines (laoairlines.com).

From China there are three overland possibilities. The Beijing–Hanoi train enters Vietnam at Dong Dang, north of Lang Son, where there's also a road crossing known as Huu Nghi Quan. The border is also open to foot traffic at Lao Cai in the northwest and Mong Cai in the far northeast.

From Laos, six border crossings are currently open to foreigners: Lao Bao, the easiest and most popular, some 80km west of Dong Ha; Cau Treo and Nam Can, to the north and northwest of Vinh; Na Meo, northwest of Thanh Hoa; Bo Y, northwest of Kon Tum; and Tay

Trang, just west of Dien Bien Phu. While it's perfectly possible – and cheaper – to use local buses to and from the borders, international bus services also run from Savannakhet and Vientiane to Hanoi, Dong Ha, Vinh, Da Nang and other destinations in Vietnam: these direct services are recommended, as regular reports of extortion continue to come in from those crossing independently.

From Cambodia you can travel by air-conditioned bus ($9–14) from Phnom Penh straight through to Ho Chi Minh City, via the Moc Bai crossing. Cheaper operators charge half these prices, but use old buses and usually get you to switch at the border. Many tour companies in Phnom Penh will be able to organize boat-plus-bus services, which are a fun way to cross the border. There are two crossings in the Mekong Delta area – Vinh Xuong and Tinh Bien, which are respectively 30km north and 25km west of Chau Doc. There are also border crossings at Xa Xia, on the coast west of the delta, which is useful if you are coming from Kep or Sihanoukville on the Cambodian coast; and at Le Thanh in the central highlands, making it possible to go from Banlung in northeast Cambodia straight through to Pleiku.

As long as you have a valid visa, crossing these borders is generally not a problem, though you may still find the odd Vietnamese immigration official who tries to charge a "processing fee", typically one dollar. Most border gates are open from around 7am to 5pm and may close for an hour over lunch.

Organized tours

If you want to cover a lot of ground in a short time in Vietnam or have a specific interest, an organized tour might be worth considering. Specialist tour operators offer packages that typically include flights, accommodation, day excursions and internal travel by plane, train or road. These are expensive compared to what you'd pay if you arranged everything independently, but the more intrepid tours often feature activities that would be difficult to set up yourself. There's a wide variety of all-inclusive packages available, as well as organized tours that cover everything from hill-tribe visits to trekking and biking. Tours range in length from a few days to several weeks, and you can choose to explore Vietnam only, or combine a tour with Laos and Cambodia.

Alternatively, you can make arrangements through local tour operators in Ho Chi Minh City, Hanoi and other tourist centres either before you arrive or on the ground; they'll arrange your entire trip or just the first few days to get you started. Fixing it up before you arrive saves time, though all local operators will also arrange an itinerary for you on the spot.

Prices will be generally cheaper with a local operator and they should have more in-depth local knowledge. However, you'll need to check carefully that they're financially sound, reliable and can deliver what they promise – never deal with a company that demands cash upfront or refuses to accept payment by credit card, and get references if you can. Also check carefully before booking to make sure you know exactly what's included in the price.

There are a fair number of excellent Vietnam-based operators; most are based in Ho Chi Minh City and Hanoi.

Getting around in Vietnam

Though still a little rough around the edges, Vietnam's transport network is continuing to improve. Most travel takes place on the roads, which are largely of decent quality surface-wise. The vehicles themselves are also pretty good, with air-conditioned coaches ferrying tourists (and an increasing number of locals) up and down Highway 1, a desperately narrow and shockingly busy thoroughfare that runs from Hanoi to Ho Chi Minh City, passing through Hué, Da Nang and Nha Trang en route. Off the main routes the vehicles are less salubrious. Trains run alongside Highway 1, and their sleeper berths are far more comfortable than buses for longer journeys. Lastly, the domestic flight network continues to evolve, and the cheap, comfortable services may save you days' worth of travel by road or rail. That said, there's plenty of room for improvement, particularly as regards road transport.

By road

Vietnam's busy, narrow roads were simply not built for overtaking, yet almost each and every vehicle is either overtaking or being overtaken at any given point – accidents are common.

Vietnam was once famed for bus drivers ripping off foreigners and cramming as many bodies as possible into their vehicles, but this is dying down; most routes now have tickets with fixed prices, and the advent of luxury "open-tour" buses on the main tourist trail saw comfort levels rocket. On the longer stretches, many buses are sleeper-berth for their whole length, though getting forty winks can be tough – the nature of local roads means that emergency stops are common, and Vietnamese drivers use their horn liberally, which can become grating very quickly on a long journey.

Security remains an important consideration. Never fall asleep with your bag by your side, and never leave belongings unattended.

By plane

Flying comes into its own on longer hauls, and can save precious hours or even days off journeys – the two-hour journey between

Hanoi and Ho Chi Minh City, for instance, compares favorably with the thirty to forty hours you would spend on the train. Prices are reasonable at around 950,000 with Jetstar, and a little more with Vietnam Airlines. Other useful services from Hanoi and Ho Chi Minh City fly to Hué, Da Nang, Nha Trang, and Phu Quoc Island. Note that you'll need your passport with you when taking internal flights.

The Vietnamese national carrier, Vietnam Airlines, operates a reasonably cheap, efficient and comprehensive network of domestic flights. The company maintains booking offices in all towns and cities with an airport; addresses and phone numbers are listed throughout the Guide.

Competition is keeping prices low on domestic flights; the aforementioned Jetstar now rival Vietnam Airlnes for local coverage, while 2009 startup Air Mekong (airmekong.com.vn) fly from Hanoi and Ho Chi Minh City to all major airports in the south of the country. Vasco (vasco.com.vn) also fly from Ho Chi Minh City to Con Dao and Ca Mau, but it's better to book through their codeshare partner Vietnam Airlines (and actually far better to go with Air Mekong's superior planes on the Con Dao route).

By rail

Given the amazing prices and regular services of the open-tour buses, few travelers opt for the train. However, rail journeys are well worth considering, for several reasons. Firstly, major roads tend to be lined in their entirety with ramshackle cafés, petrol pumps, snack stands and mobile phone shops; from the train, you'll actually see a bit of the countryside. Secondly, you'll be involved in far fewer near-collisions with trucks, motorbikes or dogs. Thirdly, you're almost guaranteed to get talking to a bunch of friendly locals – and perhaps get to join in on the feasts that some of them bring on board.

Vietnam Railways (vr.com.vn) runs a single-track train network comprising more than 2500km of line, stretching from Ho Chi Minh City to the Chinese border. Much of it dates back to the colonial period, though it's gradually being upgraded. Most of the services are still relatively slow, but travelling by train can be far more pleasant than going by road – though prices on the coastal route can't compare with buses, you're away from the busy (and often dangerous) Highway 1, and get to see far more of the countryside. Keep a particularly close eye on your belongings on the trains, and be especially vigilant when the train stops at stations, ensure your money belt is safely tucked under your clothes before going to sleep and that your luggage is safely stowed.

The most popular routes with tourists are the shuttle from Da Nang to Hué (2–3hr), a picturesque sampler of Vietnamese rail travel and the overnighters from Hué to Hanoi (11–16hr) and from Hanoi up to Lao Cai, for Sa Pa (8–9hr).

Services

The country's main line shadows Highway 1 on its way from Ho Chi Minh City to Hanoi, passing through Nha Trang, Da Nang and Hué en route. From Hanoi, three branch lines strike out towards the northern coast and Chinese border. One line traces the Red River northwest to Lao Cai, just an hour by bus from Sa Pa and also the site of a border crossing into China's Yunnan Province; unfortunately, the rail on the Chinese side is not in use. Another runs north to Dong Dang; this is the route taken by trains linking Hanoi and Beijing. The third branch, a shorter spur, links the capital with Hai Phong.

Five Reunification Express services depart daily from Hanoi to Ho Chi Minh City and vice versa, a journey that takes somewhere between thirty and forty hours. Most services arrive between 3am and 5am in both Hanoi and Ho Chi Minh City.

On the northern lines, four trains per day make the run from Hanoi to Hai Phong (2hr 30min) and two to Dong Dang (6hr). There are also four night trains (7–8hr) and a day service (9hr) to Lao Cai.

Trains usually leave on schedule from their departure points, and though delays can stack up further down the line, they're rarely too severe. Note that the only truly reliable way to learn the schedule is by checking those printed on the station wall.

Classes

When it comes to choosing which class to travel in, it's essential to aim high. At the bottom of the scale is a hard seat, which is just as it sounds, though bearable for shorter journeys; the carriages, however, tend to be filthy and since the windows are caged, views are poor and one can actually feel like an animal. Soft seats offer more comfort, especially in the new air-conditioned carriages, some of which are double-decker; the newer berths, unfortunately, tend to have flat screen TVs operating at an ear-splitting volume. On overnight journeys, you'd be well advised to invest in a berth of some description, though since the country's rolling stock is being upgraded it's not always possible to know exactly what you're getting. The new hard-berth compartments are now quite comfortable and have six bunks, three either side – the cramped top ones are the cheapest, and the bottom ones the priciest – though some of the old hard-as-nails relics remain in service. Roomier soft-berth compartments, containing only four bunks, are always comfortable.

Note that luxury carriages are attached to regular services on a couple of routes from Hanoi. Those on trains to Hué and Da Nang are operated by Livitrans (livitrans.com), and to Lao Cai by an assortment of companies.

Facilities

All Reunification Express trains now have air-conditioning, as do the overnight Lao Cai trains which have been upgraded with luxury soft-sleeper carriages. All trains are theoretically non-smoking; the rules are obeyed, by and large, in the sleeper rooms, though in hard-seat class, even the guards will be puffing away.

All train carriages have toilets, though again, it's hard to know what to expect. Most are fine, if a little grubby, though many are squat in nature; the latter are far more likely to be dirty, and to be devoid of paper or running water. Those in the soft sleeper carriages are proper sit-down toilets, and are comparatively clean.

Simple meals are often included in the price of the ticket, but you might want to stock up with goodies of your own. You'll also have plenty of opportunities to buy snacks when the train pulls into stations – and from carts that ply the aisles.

Tickets

Booking ahead is wise, and the further ahead the better, especially if you intend travelling at the weekend or a holiday period (when the lower sleeper berths are often sold as six seats, resulting in chaos). Sleeping compartments should be booked at least a day or two before departure, and even further ahead for soft-sleeper berths on the Hanoi–Hué and Hanoi–Lao Cai routes. It's not possible to buy through tickets and break your journey en route; each journey requires you to buy a separate ticket from the point of departure. Getting tickets is usually pretty painless at the station, though hotels and travel agencies will be able to book for a fee – sometimes as low as 50,000, though often much more.

Fares vary according to the class of travel and the train you take; as a rule of thumb, the faster the train, the more expensive it is. Prices (which are always quoted in dong) change regularly, but as an indication of the fare range, on the most expensive services from Hanoi to Ho Chi Minh City you'll pay around 1,500,000? for a soft-sleeper berth, and around 1,250,000? for a hard sleeper in the slowest trains; the equivalent fares for Hanoi to Hué are 750,000? and 650,000 respectively. Prices to Lao Cai vary from 80,000? for a hard seat on the day train to over 300,000? for a soft sleeper.

By bus

Most travelers use buses to get around Vietnam but never actually see a bus station. This is because the lion's share of tourist journeys are made on privately operated services, usually referred to as "open-tour" buses, which usually operate not from stations but the offices of the companies in question. The term comes from the fact that such companies typically sell through-tickets between Ho Chi Minh City and Hanoi, with customers free to stop off for as long as they like at the main points en route – Da Lat, Mui Ne, Nha Trang, Hoi An, Da Nang, Hué and Ninh Binh. There are, however, drawbacks to doing this.

Away from these private affairs, national bus services link all major cities in Vietnam, and most minor towns too, though travelers only tend to use them off the open-tour route – open-tour buses have air-conditioning, limited seating and fixed timetables, which instantly gives them the edge over national services. In addition, the fact that they don't pick up on route makes them faster too, and competition is so fierce that prices are almost as low as the national bus network.

Open-tour buses

On the whole, open-tour buses are a reasonably comfortable way to get around Vietnam; these buses also call at the occasional tourist sight, such as the Marble Mountains and Lang Co, which can save considerable time and money when compared to doing the same thing independently. Buses are usually quite decent, but don't expect too much leg-room, or any on-board toilets; some of the more expensive services have them, but the vast majority will pull in every few hours for a combined loo-and-snack break. This tends to be at mediocre and overpriced restaurants; it's a good idea to arm yourself with snacks before your journey. Another downside to open-tour buses is that you'll be encouraged to book into the company's own or affiliated hotels (usually right next to the drop-off point), though there's nothing to stop you staying elsewhere.

Services tend to run on time, and on longer trips, some take place overnight. Most of the overnight buses are filled with sleeper berths, which sounds nice and comfortable, but these are Vietnamese roads, and Vietnamese drivers – don't expect to get too much sleep. Also note that some operators are more reliable than others; Mai Linh and Hoang Long have good reputations, though some other operators have very poor standards of service.

Ticket prices vary widely depending upon which company you choose, and (if you're booking a through-ticket) how many stops you'd like to make en route; sample prices are $35 and up from Ho Chi Minh City to Hanoi, $25 from Ho Chi Minh City to Hué, and $5 from Hué to Hoi An. You can either make firm bookings at the outset or opt for an open-dated ticket for greater flexibility, in which case you may need to book your onward travel one or two days in advance to be sure of a seat. Alternatively, you can buy separate tickets as you go along, which is recommended. Each main town on the itinerary has an agent (one for each operator) where you can buy tickets and make onward reservations. To avoid being sold a fake ticket or paying over the odds, it's best to buy direct from the relevant agent rather than from hotels, restaurants or unrelated tour companies.

Other buses

On the national bus network, the government is slowly upgrading state buses, replacing the rickety old vehicles with air-conditioned models, particularly on the more popular routes. It's not uncommon to find yourself crammed in amongst the luggage, which could be anything from live pigs in baskets to scores of sacks of rice. Progress can be agonizingly slow as buses stop frequently to pick up passengers or for meal breaks. Among older vehicles, breakdowns are fairly common and can sometimes necessitate a roadside wait of several hours while driver, fare collector and mechanic roll up their sleeves and improvise a repair.

Tickets are best bought at bus stations, where fares are clearly indicated above the ticket windows. Prices are usually also marked on the tickets themselves, though there are still occasional cases of tourists being charged over the odds, particularly in more rural destinations – especially those from the Lao border. For long journeys, buy your ticket a day in advance since many routes are heavily oversubscribed.

Privately owned minibuses compete with public buses on most routes; they sometimes share the local bus station, or simply congregate on the roadside in the center of a town. You can also flag them down on the road. If anything, they squeeze in even more people per square foot than ordinary buses, and often drive interminably around town, touting for passengers. On the other hand, they do at least run throughout the day, and serve some routes not covered by public services. Such services are ticketless, so try to find what the correct fare should be and agree a price before boarding – having the right change will also come in handy. You may also find yourself dumped at the side of the road before reaching your destination, and having to cram onto the next passing service.

Most major cities have their own local bus networks, though prices and standards vary. Try to ascertain the correct price and have the exact money ready before boarding as fare collectors will often take advantage of your captive position.

By ferry and boat

A boat-tour around Ha Long Bay is one of Vietnam's most enjoyable trips, while scheduled ferries sail year-round – weather permitting – to the major islands off Vietnam's coastline, including Phu Quoc, Cat Ba and Con Dao. In addition, ferry and hydrofoil services run from Hai Phong to Cat Ba, and hydrofoils from Ho Chi Minh City to Vung Tau, and from Ha Long City to Mong Cai and Bai Tu Long. Though they are gradually being replaced by bridges, a few river ferries still haul themselves from bank to bank of the various strands of the Mekong from morning until night.

By car and jeep

Self-drive in Vietnam is not yet an option for tourists and other short-term visitors. However, it's easy to rent a car, jeep or minibus with driver from the same companies, agencies and tourist offices that arrange tours. This can be quite an economical means of transport if you are travelling in a group. Moreover, it means you can plan a trip to your own tastes, rather than having to follow a tour company's itinerary.

Prices vary wildly so it pays to shop around, but expect to pay in the region of $50 per day for a car, and $90 per day for a jeep or other 4WD, depending on the vehicle's size, age and level of comfort. When negotiating the price, it's important to clarify exactly who is liable for what. Things to check include who pays for the driver's accommodation and meals, fuel, road and ferry tolls, parking fees and repairs and what happens in the case of a major breakdown. There should then be some sort of contract to sign showing all the details, including an agreed itinerary, especially if you are renting for more than a day; make sure the driver is given a copy in Vietnamese. In some cases, you'll have to settle up in advance, though, if possible, it's best if you can arrange to pay roughly half before and the balance at the end.

By motorbike

Motorbike rental is possible in most towns and cities regularly frequented by tourists, and pottering around on one can be an enjoyable and time-efficient method of sightseeing. Lured by the prospect of independent travel at relatively low cost, some tourists cruise the countryside on motorbikes, but inexperienced bikers would do well to think very hard before undertaking any long-distance biking since Vietnam's roads can be distinctly dangerous.

The appalling road discipline of most Vietnamese drivers means that the risk of an accident is very real, with potentially dire consequences should it happen in a remote area. Well-equipped hospitals are few and far between outside the major centres, and there'll probably be no ambulance service.

On the other hand, many people ride around with no problems and thoroughly recommend it for both day-trips and touring. The best biking is to be found in the northern mountains, the central highlands and around the Mekong Delta, while the Ho Chi Minh Highway offers pristine tarmac plus wonderful scenery. Some also do the long haul up Highway 1 from Ho Chi Minh City to Hanoi (or vice versa), a journey of around two weeks, averaging a leisurely 150km per day.

There's no shortage of motorbikes for rent in Vietnam's major tourist centres; the average rate is around $7 per day, with discounts for longer periods. You'll sometimes be asked to pay in advance, sign a rental contract and/or leave some form of ID (a photocopy of your passport should suffice). If you're renting for a week or so, you may be asked to leave a deposit, often the bike's value in dollars though it might also be your air ticket or departure card. In the vast majority of cases, this shouldn't be a problem.

Although it's technically illegal for non-residents to own a vehicle, there's a small trade in secondhand motorbikes in the two main cities – look at the noticeboards in hotels, travelers' cafés and tour agents for adverts. So far the police have ignored the practice, but check the latest situation before committing yourself. The bike of choice is usually a Minsk 125cc, particularly for the mountains; it's sturdy, not too expensive, and the easiest to get repaired outside the main cities.

Whether you're renting or buying, remember to check everything over carefully, especially brakes, lights and horn. Wearing a helmet is now a legal requirement, and most rental outlets have helmets you can borrow, sometimes for a small charge, though they may not be top-quality.

Note that international driving licenses are not valid in Vietnam, but you will need your home driving license and bike registration papers. You also need at least third-party insurance, which is available (with the aforementioned documentation) at Bao Viet insurance offices.

Though road conditions have improved remarkably in recent years, off the main highways they can still be highly erratic, with pristine asphalt followed by stretches of spine-jarring potholes, and plenty of loose gravel on the sides of the road. Repair shops are fairly ubiquitous – ask for sua chua xe may (motorbike repairs) – but you should still carry at least a puncture-repair kit, pump and spare spark plug. Fuel (xang) is cheap and widely available at the roadsides, often from bottles. Finally, try to travel in the company of one or more other bikes in case one of you gets into trouble. And if you want to get off the main highways, it really pays to take a guide.

By bicycle

Cycling is an excellent way of sightseeing around towns, and you shouldn't have to pay more than 50,000 per day for the privilege, even outside the main tourist centres.

While you can now buy decent Japanese-made bikes in Vietnam, if you decide on a long-distance cycling holiday, you should really bring your own bike with you, not forgetting all the necessary spares and tools. Hardy mountain bikes cope best with the country's variable surfaces, though tourers and hybrids are fine on the main roads. Bring your own helmet and a good loud bell; a rear-view mirror also comes in handy.

When it all gets too much, or you want to skip between towns, you can always put your bike on the train (though not on all services; check when buying your ticket) for a small fee; take it to the station well ahead of time, where it will be packed and placed in the luggage van. Some open-tour buses will also take bikes – free if it goes in the luggage hold (packed up), otherwise you'll have to pay for an extra seat.

If you want to see Vietnam from the saddle, there are several companies that offer specialist cycling tours. In addition to a few of the international tour operators, there are local outfits such as Phat Tire (phattireventures.com).

Organized tours

Ever-increasing numbers of tourists are seeing Vietnam through the window of a minibus, on organized tours. Ranging from one-day jaunts to two- or three-week trawls upcountry, tours are ideal if you want to acquaint yourself speedily with the highlights of Vietnam; they can also work out much cheaper than car rental. On the other hand, by relying upon tours you'll have little chance to really get to grips with the country and its people, or to enjoy things at your leisure.

Hordes of state-owned and private tour companies compete for business – see our lists of well-established agents in Ho Chi Minh City and Hanoi. While a few companies now put together more innovative itineraries, the vast majority offer similar tours. However, it pays to shop around since prices vary wildly depending, for example, on how many people there are in a group, the standard of transport, meals and accommodation, whether entry fees are included and so forth.

It's important to check exactly what is included in the price before handing over any cash. It's also a good idea to ask about the maximum number of people on the trip and whether your group will be amalgamated with others if you don't want to be travelling round in a great horde. Bear in mind, as well, that you're far better off dealing directly with the company organizing the tour, rather than going through a hotel or other intermediary. Not only are you more likely to get accurate information about the details of the tour, but you'll also be in a much stronger position should you have cause for complaint.

The other alternative is to set up your own custom-made tour by gathering together a group and renting a car, jeep or minibus plus driver.

Local transport

In a country with a population so adept at making do with limited resources, it isn't surprising to see the diverse types of local transport. While taxis are increasingly common and a number of cities now boast reasonable bus services, elsewhere you'll be reliant on a host of two- and three-wheeled vehicles for getting around.

Most common by far are motorbike taxis known as xe om. In the cities you'll rarely be able to walk twenty yards without being offered a ride; prices tend to start at around 10,000 for very short runs, though this goes up after dark (as does the possibility of extortion). At all times the rules of bargaining apply: when haggling, ensure you know which currency you are dealing in (five fingers held up, for instance, could mean 5000, 50,000 or 5), and whether you're negotiating for a single or return trip, and for one passenger or two; it's always best to write the figures down. Should a difference of opinion emerge at the end of a ride, having the exact fare ready to press into an argumentative driver's hand can sometimes resolve matters.

Xe om have almost entirely replaced that quintessential Vietnamese mode of transport, the cyclo. These three-wheeled rickshaws comprising a "bucket" seat attached to the front of a bicycle can carry one person, or two people at a push, and are now only really found in tourist areas (though locals use them just as much as foreigners). Prices vary by area, and there are continuous stories of cyclo drivers charging outrageous sums for their services, so to avoid getting badly ripped off, find out first what a reasonable fare might be from your hotel; if the first driver won't agree to your offer, simply walk on and try another.

Taxis are now a common sight on the streets of all major cities. The vast majority are metered (with prices in dong) and fares are not expensive; a short ride within central Hanoi, for example, should cost around 30,000. Though standards have been improving with greater competition, some drivers need persuading to use their meters, while others dawdle along as the meter spins suspiciously fast, or take you on an unnecessarily long route. When arriving in a town, beware of drivers who insist the hotel you ask for is closed and want to take you elsewhere; this is usually a commission scam – be firm with your directions. In general, smarter-looking taxis and those waiting outside big hotels tend to be more reliable; the Mai Linh network has by far the best reputation, and you'll see their green cabs all across the land.

Accommodation

The standard of accommodation in Vietnam is, by and large, excellent. In the main tourist areas the range caters to all budgets, and though prices are a little expensive by Southeast Asian standards, the quality is generally quite high. Competition is fierce and with the construction boom still ongoing rooms are being added all the time – great for the traveler, as it keeps prices low and service standards high. There has been a massive increase in the number of luxury resorts along the coast (mainly aimed at the Asian package tour market), while budget travelers and those travelling off the tourist trail will find good budget accommodation throughout the country.

Another consequence of the number of new hotels springing up in recent years is that getting a reservation is no longer the nightmare it once was, and even among international-class hotels there are some bargains to be had, particularly at weekends; however, booking in advance is a must around the Tet festival in early spring.

Tourist booth staff at the airports in Ho Chi Minh City and Hanoi will phone to reserve a room for you, and it's increasingly simple to book online. Be wary of asking advice from cyclo or taxi drivers, as travelers are often told that their hotel of choice is full or closed. It's also important to note that Vietnam is full of copycat establishments – to avoid being taken to a similarly named hotel, write down the street name and show it to your driver.

Once you've found a hotel, look at a range of rooms before opting for one, as standards can vary hugely within the same establishment. You'll also need to check the bed arrangement, since there are many permutations in Vietnam. A "single" room could have a single or twin beds in it, while a "double" room could have two, three or four single beds, a double, a single and a double, and so on.

When you check in at a Vietnamese hotel or guesthouse, you'll be asked for your passport, which is needed for registration with the local authorities. Depending on the establishment, these will be either returned to you the same night, or kept as security until you check out. If you're going to lose sleep over being separated from your passport, say you need it for the bank; many places will accept photocopies of your picture and visa pages. It's normally possible to pay your bill when you leave, although a few budget places ask for payment in advance.

Room rates fluctuate according to demand, so it's always worth bargaining – making sure, of course, that it's clear whether both parties are talking per person or per room. Your case will be that much stronger if you are staying several nights.

All hotels charge 10 percent government tax, while top-class establishments also add a service charge (typically 5 percent). These taxes may or may not be included in the room rate, so check to be sure. Increasingly, breakfast is included in the price of all but the cheapest rooms; in budget places it will consist of little more than bread with jam or cheese and a cup of tea or coffee, while those splashing out a little more may be greeted by a gigantic morning buffet. Prices given in the guide are based on those found at the time of writing for the cheapest double room. Prices are often quoted in dong, which have been converted to dollars at the rate as it was at the time of going to press. However, because of the extreme volatility of the exchange rate (which can change by hundreds or thousands of dong each week), these prices are subject to constant change.

Although the situation is improving, hotel security can be a problem. Never leave valuables lying about in your room and keep documents, travelers' cheques and so forth with you at all times, in a money pouch. While top-end and many mid-range hotels provide safety deposit boxes, elsewhere you can sometimes leave things in a safe or locked drawer at reception; put everything in a sealed envelope and ask for a receipt. In the real cheapies, where the door may only be secured with a padlock, you can increase security by using your own lock.

In some older budget hotels, rooms are cleaned irregularly and badly, and hygiene can be a problem, with cockroaches and even rats roaming free; you can at least minimize health risks by not bringing foodstuffs or sugary drinks into your room.

Pretty much any guesthouse or hotel will offer a laundry service, and Western-style laundry and dry-cleaning services are widely available in Hanoi, Ho Chi Minh City and other major cities. Washing is often given a rigorous scrubbing by hand, so don't submit anything delicate.

Finally, prostitution is rife in Vietnam, and in less reputable hotels it's not unknown for Western men to be called upon, or even phoned from other rooms, during the night.

Types of accommodation

Grading accommodation isn't a simple matter in Vietnam. The names used (guesthouse, mini-hotel, hotel and so on) can rarely be relied upon to indicate what's on offer, and there are broad overlaps in standards. Vietnam's older hotels tend to be austere, state-owned edifices styled upon unlovely Eastern European models, while many private mini-hotels make a real effort. Some hotels cover all bases by having a range of rooms, from simple fan-cooled rooms with cold water, right up to cheerful air-conditioned accommodation with satellite TV, fridge and mini-bar. As a rule of thumb, the newer a place is, the better value it's likely to represent in terms of comfort, hygiene and all-round appeal.

There are a burgeoning number of "resorts" appearing across the country. In contrast to the Western image of an all-inclusive complex, in Vietnam these are simply hotels, usually with pretty landscaped gardens, located on the beach or in the countryside. All that's included in the rate is breakfast, though it is possible to eat all your meals here.

Budget accommodation

The very cheapest form of accommodation in Vietnam is a bed in a dormitory, though as yet, very few cities have such facilities – there are dedicated hostels in Hanoi, Ho Chi Minh City and Hué, where you can expect to pay from about $6 for a bed, sharing common facilities. Do note that though most of these have private rooms, you'll pay less elsewhere. In the two main cities there are also a fair few budget guesthouses equipped with "backpacker" dorms – you'll generally find these around the De Tham enclave in Ho Chi Minh City, and the Old Quarter in Hanoi (see the respective chapters for more). In Hanoi there is also a small network of youth hostels fully accredited by Hostelling International (hihostels.com); you'll need a current Youth Hostel card, which you can buy when checking in.

If you prefer your own privacy, you'll find simple fan rooms in either a guesthouse or hotel (khach san), with prices starting at around $10; these are likely to be en-suite, although you might not get hot water at this price level in the warmer south. Add air-conditioning, satellite TV and slightly better furnishings, maybe even a window, and you'll be paying up to $20. Upgrading to $20–30 will get you a larger room with better-standard fittings, usually including a fridge and bathtub, and possibly a balcony. Note that while many hotels advertise satellite TV, which channels you actually get varies wildly, let alone the quality of reception, so check first if it matters to you.

Mid- and upper-range accommodation

For upwards of $30 per room per night, accommodation can begin to get quite rosy. Rooms at this level will be comfortable, reasonably spacious and well-appointed with decent furniture, air-conditioning, hot water, fridge, phone and satellite TV in all but the most remote areas.

Paying $30–75 will get you a room in a mid-range hotel of some repute, with in-house restaurant and bar, booking office, room service and so on. At the top of the range the sky's the limit. Most of the international-class hotels are located in the two major cities, which also have some reasonably charismatic places to stay, such as the Metropole in Hanoi and Ho Chi Minh's Continental. However, in recent years developers have targeted Nha Trang, Hoi An, Da Nang and Ha Long City, all of which now boast upmarket resort hotels. Off the main trail, there's usually one or two upper-range hotels in each main city, though very few exist in the countryside.

Village accommodation and camping

As Vietnam's minority communities have become more exposed to tourism, staying in stilt houses or other village accommodation has become more feasible.

In the north of the country, notably around Sa Pa and in the Mai Chau Valley, you can either take one of the tours out of Hanoi which includes a home-stay in one of the minority villages, or make your own arrangements when you get there. In the central highlands, the Pleiku and Kon Tum tourist offices can also arrange a stilt house home-stay for you.

Accommodation usually consists of a mattress on the floor in a communal room. Those villages more used to tourists normally provide a blanket and mosquito net, but it's advisable to take your own net and sleeping bag to be on the safe side, particularly as nights get pretty cold in the mountains. Prices in the villages vary from $5–15 per person per night, depending on the area and whether meals are included.

Where boat trips operate in the Mekong Delta, notably around Vinh Long, tour operators in Ho Chi Minh City or the local tourist board can arrange for visitors to stay with owners of fruit orchards, allowing a close-up view of rural life.

Virtually no provisions exist in Vietnam for camping at the present time. The exceptions are at Nha Trang and Mui Ne, where some guesthouses offer tents for a few dollars a night when all rooms are full. Some tour companies also offer camping as an option when visiting Ha Long Bay.

Food & Drink

Internationally speaking, Thai food may be the most heralded of all the Southeast Asian cuisines, but true connoisseurs would go for Vietnamese every time. Light, subtle in flavor and astonishing in their variety, Vietnamese dishes are boiled or steamed rather than stir-fried, and a huge emphasis is placed on herbs and seasoning – no great surprise in this land of diverse climates.

In the south, Indian and Thai influences add curries and spices to the menu, while other regions have evolved their own array of specialties, most notably the foods of Hué and Hoi An. Buddhism introduced a vegetarian tradition to Vietnam, while much later the French brought with them bread, dairy products, pastries and the whole café culture. Hanoi, Ho Chi Minh City and the major tourist centres are now well provided with everything from street hawkers to hotel and Western-style restaurants, and even ice-cream parlors; in such places, you'll also find a few restaurants putting on cooking classes.

The quality and variety of food is generally better in the main towns than off the beaten track, where restaurants of any sort are few and far between. That said, you'll never go hungry; even in the back of beyond, there's always some stall selling a noodle soup or rice platter and plenty of fruit to fill up on.

Vietnam's national drink is green tea, which is the accompaniment to every social gathering or business meeting and is frequently drunk after meals. At the harder end of the spectrum, there's also rice wine, though some local beer is also excellent, and an increasingly wide range of imported wines and spirits.

Where to eat

Broadly speaking, there are two types of eating establishment to choose from. One step up from hawkers peddling their dish of the day from shoulder poles or handcarts are street kitchens – inexpensive joints aimed at locals. More formal, Western-style restaurants come in many shapes and sizes, from simple places serving unpretentious Vietnamese meals to top-class establishments offering high quality Vietnamese specialties and international cuisine.

While most eating establishments stay open throughout the year, some close over Tet. The Vietnamese eat early: outside the major cities and tourist areas; food stalls and street kitchens rarely stay open beyond 8pm and may close even earlier, though they do stay open later in the south, especially in Ho Chi Minh City. You'll need to brush up your chopstick-handling skills, too, although other utensils are always available in places frequented by tourists – in Western-style restaurants you won't be expected to tackle your steak-frites with chopsticks.

When it comes to paying, the normal sign language will be readily understood in most restaurants. In street kitchens you pay as you leave – either proffer a few thousand dong to signal your intentions, or ask bao nhieu tien? ("how much is it?"). As with accommodation, prices are listed in dollars throughout the guide but exchange rates may be wildly different by the time you travel and the smaller, local establishments often prefer to be paid in dong.

Street kitchens

Eating on the street may not be to every visitor's taste, but those willing to take the plunge usually put it up among their favorite experiences in the country – the food is often better in quality to that found at restaurants, it's much cheaper, and a whole lot more fun. Street kitchens range from makeshift food stalls, set up on the street around a cluster of pint-size stools, to eating houses where, as often as not, the cooking is still done on the street but you either sit in an open-fronted dining area or join the overspill outside. Both tend to have fixed locations, though only the eating houses will have an address – which usually doubles as their name. Some places stay open all day (7am–8pm), while many close once they've run out of ingredients and others only open at lunchtime (10.30am–2pm). To be sure of the widest choice and freshest food, it pays to get there early (as early as 11.30am at lunchtime, and by 7pm in the evening), and note that the best places will be packed around noon.

Most specialize in one type of food, generally indicated (in Vietnamese only) on a signboard outside, or offer the ubiquitous com (rice dishes) and pho (noodle soups). Com binh dan, "people's meals", are also popular. Here you select from an array of prepared dishes displayed in a glass cabinet or on a buffet table, piling your plate with such things as stuffed tomatoes, fried fish, tofu, pickles or eggs, plus a helping of rice; expect to pay from around 25,000? for a good plateful. Though it's not a major problem at these prices, some street kitchens overcharge, so double-check when ordering.

Though eating street food is highly recommended, it's worth using a bit of judicious selection – look for places with a fast turnover, where the ingredients are obviously fresh. A bit of basic vocabulary will certainly help.

In a similar vein to street kitchens are bia hoi outlets. Though these are primarily drinking establishments, many provide good-value snacks or even main meals.

Restaurants

If you're after more relaxed dining, where people aren't queuing for your seat, then head for a Western-style Vietnamese restaurant (nha hang), which will have chairs rather than stools, a name, a menu and will often be closed to the street. In general, these places serve a more varied selection of Vietnamese dishes than the street kitchens, plus a smattering of international – generally European – dishes.

Menus at this level usually show prices, particularly in areas popular with tourists. If there are no prices on your menu, confirm them with staff before you start eating to avoid any potential overcharging issues. Prices vary considerably depending upon what you order, but you'll get a modest meal for less than $5 per head. Opening hours at such places are usually from 10.30am to 2pm for lunch, and in the evening from 5pm to no later than 9pm, or 8pm in the north.

In the main tourist haunts, you'll find cheap and cheerful cafés aimed at the backpacker market and serving often mediocre Western and Vietnamese dishes – from burgers and banana pancakes to spring rolls, noodles and other Vietnamese standards. They have the advantage, however, of all-day opening, usually from 7am to 11pm or midnight. And, should you crave a reasonably priced Western-style breakfast, fresh fruit salad or a mango shake, these are the places to go.

As you move up the price scale, the decor and the cuisine become more sophisticated and the menu more varied. The more expensive restaurants (including the smarter hotel dining rooms) tend to stay open later in the evening, perhaps until 9.30pm or 10.30pm. Some have menus priced in dollars, and more and more accept credit cards. Usually menus indicate if there's a service charge, but watch out for an additional 3–4 percent on credit card payments. These restaurants can be relatively fancy places, with at least a nod towards decor and ambience, and correspondingly higher prices (a meal for two is likely to cost at least $20 and often much more).

The most popular foreign cuisine on offer is French, though both Hanoi and Ho Chi Minh City boast some pretty good international restaurants, including Thai, Chinese, Tex Mex, Indian and Italian. You'll find these international cuisines, and upper-class Vietnamese restaurants, in Hanoi, Ho Chi Minh City, Hué, Da Nang, Hoi An and Nha Trang, though they're scarce in the rest of the country.

Vietnamese food

The staple of Vietnamese meals is rice, with noodles a popular alternative at breakfast or as a snack. Typically, rice will be accompanied by a fish or meat dish, a vegetable dish and soup, followed by a green tea digestive. Seafood and fish – from rivers, lakes, canals and paddy fields as well as the sea – are favored throughout the country, either fresh or dried. The most commonly used flavorings are shallots, coriander and lemon grass. Ginger, saffron, mint, anise and a basil-type herb also feature strongly, and coconut milk gives some southern dishes a distinctive richness.

Even in the south, Vietnamese food tends not to be over-spicy; instead chili sauces or fresh chilies are served separately. Vietnam's most famous seasoning is the ubiquitous nuoc mam, a nutrient-packed sauce which either is added during cooking or forms the base for various dipping sauces. Nuoc mam is made by fermenting huge quantities of fish in vats of salt for between six months and a year, after which the dark brown liquid is strained and graded according to its age and flavor. Foreigners usually find the smell of the sauce pretty rank, but most soon acquire a taste for its distinctive salty-sweetness.

The use of monosodium glutamate (MSG) can be excessive, especially in northern cooking, and some people are known to react badly to the seasoning. A few restaurants in the main cities have cottoned on to the foibles of foreigners and advertise MSG-free food; elsewhere, try saying khong co my chinh (without MSG), and keep your fingers crossed. Note that what looks like salt on the table is sometimes MSG, so taste it first.

The most famous Vietnamese dish has to be spring rolls, variously known as cha gio, cha nem, nem ran or just plain nem. Various combinations of minced pork, shrimp or crab, rice vermicelli, onions, bean sprouts and an edible fungus are rolled in rice-paper wrappers, and then eaten fresh or deep-fried. In some places they're served with a bowl of lettuce and/or mint. In addition, a southern variation has barbecued strips of pork wrapped in semi-transparent rice wrappers, along with raw ingredients such as green banana and star fruit, and then dunked in a rich peanut sauce – every bit as tasty as it sounds.

Soups and noodles

Though it originated in the north, another dish you'll find throughout Vietnam is pho (pronounced as the British say "fur"), a noodle soup eaten at any time of day but primarily at breakfast. The basic bowl of pho consists of a light beef broth, flavored with ginger, coriander and sometimes cinnamon, to which are added broad, flat rice-noodles, spring onions and slivers of chicken, pork or beef. At the table you add a squeeze of lime and a sprinkling of chili flakes or a spoonful of chili sauce.

Countless other types of soup are dished up at street restaurants. Bun bo is another substantial beef and noodle soup eaten countrywide, though most famous in Hué; in the south, hu tieu, a soup of vermicelli, pork and seafood noodles, is best taken in My Tho. Chao (or xhao), on the other hand, is a thick rice gruel served piping hot, usually with shredded chicken or filleted fish, flavored with dill and with perhaps a raw egg cooking at the bottom; it's often served with fried breadsticks (quay). Sour soups are a popular accompaniment for fish, while lau, a standard in local restaurants, is more of a main meal than a soup, where the vegetable broth arrives at the table in a steamboat (a ring-shaped metal dish on live coals or, nowadays, often electrically heated). You cook slivers of beef, prawns or similar in the simmering soup, and then drink the flavorful liquid that's left in the cooking pot.

Fish and meat

Among the highlights of Vietnamese cuisine are its succulent seafood and freshwater fish. Cha ca is the most famous of these dishes: white fish sautéed in butter at the table with dill and spring onions, then served with rice noodles and a sprinkling of peanuts; invented in Hanoi, it's now found in most upmarket restaurants. Another dish found in more expensive restaurants is chao tom (or tom bao mia), consisting of savoury shrimp pate wrapped round sweet sugar cane and fried. Ca kho to, fish stew cooked in a clay pot, is a southern specialty.

Every conceivable type of meat and part of the animal anatomy finds itself on the Vietnamese dining table, though the staples are straightforward beef, chicken and pork. Ground meat, especially pork, is a common constituent of stuffings, for example in spring rolls or the similar banh cuon, a steamed, rice-flour "ravioli" filled with minced pork, black mushrooms and bean sprouts; a popular variation uses prawns instead of meat. Pork is also used, with plenty of herbs, to make Hanoi's bun cha, small hamburgers barbecued on an open charcoal brazier and served on a bed of cold rice-noodles with greens and a slightly sweetish sauce. One famous southern dish is bo bay mon (often written bo 7 mon), meaning literally beef seven ways, consisting of a platter of beef cooked in different styles.

Roving gourmets may want to try some of the more unusual meats on offer. Dog meat (thit cay or thit cho) is a particular delicacy in the north, where "yellow" dogs (sandy-haired varieties) are considered the tastiest. Winter is the season to eat dog meat – it's said to give extra body heat, and is also supposed to remove bad luck if consumed at the end of the lunar month. Snake (thit con ran), like dog, is supposed to improve male virility. Dining on snake is surrounded by a ritual, which, if you're guest of honor, requires you to swallow the still-beating heart. Another one strictly for the strong of stomach is trung vit lon, embryo-containing duck eggs boiled and eaten only five days before hatching – bill, webbed feet, feathers and all.

Vegetables – and vegetarian food

If all this has put you off meat forever, it is possible to eat vegetarian food in Vietnam, though not always easy. The widest selection of vegetables is to be found in Da Lat where a staggering variety of tropical and temperate crops thrive. Elsewhere, most restaurants offer a smattering of meat-free dishes, from stewed spinach or similar greens, to a more appetizing mix of onion, tomato, bean sprouts, various mushrooms, peppers and so on; places used to foreigners may be able to oblige with vegetarian spring rolls (nem an chay or nem khong co thit). At street kitchens you're likely to find tofu and one or two dishes of pickled vegetables, such as cabbage or cucumber, while occasionally they may also have aubergine, bamboo shoots or avocado, depending on the season.

However, unless you go to a specialist vegetarian outlet – of which there are some excellent examples in Ho Chi Minh City, Hanoi and Hué – it can be a problem finding genuine veggie food: soups are usually made with beef stock, morsels of pork fat sneak into otherwise innocuous-looking dishes and animal fat tends to be used for frying.

The phrase to remember is an chay (vegetarian), or seek out a vegetarian rice shop (tiem com chay). Otherwise, make the most of the first and fifteenth days of the lunar month when many Vietnamese Buddhists spurn meat and you're more likely to find vegetarian dishes on offer.

Snacks

Vietnam has a wide range of snacks and nibbles to fill any yawning gaps, from huge rice-flour crackers sprinkled with sesame seeds to all sorts of dried fish, nuts and seeds. Banh bao are white, steamed dumplings filled with tasty titbits, such as pork, onions and tangy mushrooms or strands of sweet coconut. Banh xeo, meaning sizzling pancake, combines shrimp, pork, bean sprouts and egg, all fried and then wrapped in rice paper with a selection of greens before being dunked in a spicy sauce. A similar dish, originating from Hué – a city with a vast repertoire of snack foods – is banh khoai, in which the flat pancake is accompanied by a plate of star fruit, green banana and aromatic herbs, plus a rich peanut sauce.

Markets are often good snacking grounds, with stalls churning out soups and spring rolls or selling intriguing banana-leaf parcels of pate (a favorite accompaniment for bia hoi), pickled pork sausage or perhaps a cake of sticky rice.

A relative newcomer on the culinary scene is French bread, made with wheat flour in the north and rice flour in the south. Baguettes –

sometimes sold warm from street side stoves – are sliced open and stuffed with pate, soft cheese or ham and pickled vegetables.

Fruit

With its diverse climate, Vietnam is blessed with both tropical and temperate fruits, including dozens of banana species. The richest orchards are in the south, where pineapple, coconut, papaya, mango, longan and mangosteen flourish. Da Lat is famous for its strawberries, while the region around Nha Trang produces the peculiar "dragon fruit" (thanh long). The size and shape of a small pineapple, the dragon fruit has skin of shocking pink, studded with small protuberances, and smooth, white flesh speckled with tiny black seeds. The slightly sweet, watery flesh is thirst-quenching, and so is often served as a drink, crushed with ice.

A fruit that is definitely an acquired taste is the durian, a spiky, yellow-green football-sized fruit with an unmistakably pungent odor reminiscent of mature cheese and caramel, but tasting like an onion-laced custard. Jackfruit looks worryingly similar to durian but is larger and has smaller spikes. Its yellow segments of flesh are deliciously sweet.

Sweet things

Vietnam is not strong on desserts – restaurants usually stick to ice cream and fruit, although fancier international places might venture into tiramisu territory. Those with a sweet tooth are better off hunting down a bakery – there'll be one within walking distance in any urban area – or browsing around street stalls where there are usually candied fruits and other Vietnamese sweetmeats on offer, as well as sugary displays of French-inspired cakes and pastries in the main tourist centres.

Green-colored banh com is an eye-catching local delicacy made by wrapping pounded glutinous rice around sugary, green-bean paste. A similar confection, found only during the mid-autumn festival, is the "earth cake", banh deo, which melds the contrasting flavors of candied fruits, sesame and lotus seeds with a dice of savoury pork fat. Fritters are popular among children and you'll find opportunistic hawkers outside schools, selling banh chuoi (banana fritters) and banh chuoi khoai (mixed slices of banana and sweet potato).

Most cities now have ice-cream parlors selling tubs or sticks of the local, hard ices in chocolate, vanilla or green-tea flavors, though it's prudent to buy only from the larger, busier outlets and not from street hawkers. More exotic tastes can be satisfied at the European- and American-style ice-cream parlors of Hanoi and Ho Chi Minh City, while excellent yoghurts are also increasingly available at ice-cream parlors, and even some restaurants.

Drinks

Giai khat means "quench your thirst" and you'll see the signs everywhere, on stands selling fresh juices, bottled cold drinks or outside cafés and bia hoi (draught beer) outlets. Many drinks are served with ice: tempting though it may be, the only really safe policy is to avoid ice altogether – dung bo da, cam on ("no ice, thanks") should do the trick. That said, ice in the top hotels, bars and restaurants is generally reliable, and some people take the risk in less salubrious establishments with apparent impunity.

Water and soft drinks

Tap water is not safe to drink in Vietnam – since bottled water is both cheap and widely available, you shouldn't need to take the risk anyway. Avoid drinks with ice or those that may have been diluted with suspect water.

Locally made soft drinks are tooth-numbingly sweet, but are cheap and safe – as long as the bottle or carton appears well sealed – and on sale just about everywhere. The Coke, Sprite and Fanta hegemony also means you can find fizzy drinks in surprisingly remote areas. Oddly, canned drinks are usually more expensive than the equivalent-sized bottle, whether it's a soft drink or beer – apparently it's less chic to drink from the old-fashioned bottle.

A more effective thirst-quencher is fresh coconut juice, though this is more difficult to find in the north. Fresh juices such as orange and lime are also delicious – just make sure they haven't been mixed with tap water. Sugar-cane juice (mia da) is safer, since it's pressed right in front of you. Pasteurized milk, produced by Vinamilk, is now sold in the main towns and cities.

Somewhere between a drink and a snack, ché is made from taro flour and green bean, and served over ice with chunks of fruit, colored jellies and even sweet corn or potato. In hot weather it provides a refreshing sugar-fix.

Tea and coffee

Tea drinking is part of the social ritual in Vietnam. Small cups of refreshing, strong, green tea are presented to all guests or visitors: water is well boiled and safe to drink, as long as the cup itself is clean, and it's considered rude not to take at least a sip. Although your cup will be continually replenished to show hospitality, you don't have to carry on drinking; the polite way to decline a refill is to place your hand over the cup when your host is about to replenish it. Green tea is also served at the end of every restaurant meal, particularly in the south, and usually provided free.

Coffee production has boomed in recent years, largely for export, with serious environmental and social consequences. The Vietnamese drink coffee very strong and in small quantities, with a large dollop of condensed milk at the bottom of the cup. Traditionally, coffee is filtered at the table by means of a small dripper balanced over the cup or glass, which sometimes sits in a bowl of hot water to keep it warm. However, places accustomed to tourists increasingly run too fresh (pasteurized) milk, while in the main cities you'll now find fancy Western-style cafés turning out decent lattes and cappuccinos. Highland Coffee has become Vietnam's very own Starbucks-style chain, while out in the sticks you're best off going for cafés with a Trung Nguyen sign.

Alcoholic drinks

In Vietnam, drinking alcohol is a social activity to be shared with friends. You'll rarely see the Vietnamese drinking alone and never without eating. Be prepared for lots of toasts to health, wealth and happiness, and no doubt to international understanding, too. It's the custom to fill the glasses of your fellow guests; someone else will fill yours.

Canned and bottled beers brewed under license in Vietnam include Tiger, Heineken, Carlsberg and San Miguel, but there are also plenty of very drinkable – and cheaper – local beers around, such as Halida, 333 (Ba Ba Ba) and Bivina. Some connoisseurs rate Bière la Rue from Da Nang tops, though Saigon Export, Hanoi Beer and BGI are also fine brews. Many other towns boast their own local beers, such as Hué (where the main brand is Huda), Hai Phong and Thanh Hoa (where it's simply named after the town) – all worth a try.

Roughly forty years ago technology for making bia hoi (draught beer) was introduced from Czechoslovakia and it is now quaffed in vast quantities, particularly in the north. Bia hoi may taste fairly weak, but it measures in at up to four percent alcohol. It's also ridiculously cheap – between 2500 and 5000 a glass – and supposedly unadulterated with chemicals, so in theory you're less likely to get a hangover. Bia hoi has a 24-hour shelf life, which means the better places sell out by early evening, and that you're unlikely to be drinking it into the wee hours. In the south, you're more likely to be drinking bia tuoi ("fresh" beer), a close relation of bia hoi but served from pressurized barrels. Outlets are usually open at lunchtime, and then again in the evening from 5pm to 9pm.

Wine (the conventional kind) is becoming increasingly popular in Vietnam – even in small towns, you'll easily track some down, and imported bottles continue to crop up in the most unexpected places. Local production dates from the French era, and is centered around Da Lat – the main producer is Vang Da Lat, bottles of which will cost from 50,000 in a shop, and 70,000 at a restaurant. Only at top hotels, restaurants or specialist shops will you find decent imported bottles that have been properly stored; you'll be paying premium prices for these.

Health

Vietnam's health problems read like a dictionary of tropical medicine. Diseases that are under control elsewhere in Southeast Asia have been sustained here by poverty, dietary deficiencies, poor healthcare and the disruption caused by half a century of war. The situation is improving, however, and by coming prepared and taking a few simple precautions while in the country, you're unlikely to come down with anything worse than a cold or a dose of travelers' diarrhea.

When planning your trip, it's wise to visit a doctor as early as possible, preferably at least two months before you leave, to allow time to complete any recommended courses of vaccinations. It's also advisable to have a trouble-shooting dental check-up – and remember that you generally need to start taking anti-malarial tablets at least one week before your departure.

For up-to-the-minute information, it may be worth visiting a specialized travel clinic; most clinics also sell travel-associated accessories, including mosquito nets and first-aid kits.

Vaccinations

No vaccinations are required for Vietnam (except yellow fever if you're coming directly from an area where the disease is endemic), but typhoid and hepatitis A jabs are recommended; it's also worth ensuring you're up to date with boosters such as tetanus and polio. Additional injections to consider, depending on the season and risk of exposure, are hepatitis B, Japanese encephalitis, meningitis and rabies. All these immunizations can be obtained at international clinics in Hanoi, Ho Chi Minh City and Da Nang, but it's less hassle and usually cheaper to get them done at home. Get all your shots recorded on an International Certificate of Vaccination and carry this with your passport when travelling abroad.

For protection against hepatitis A, which is spread by contaminated food and water, the vaccine is expensive but extremely effective – an initial injection followed by a booster after six to twelve months provides immunity for up to ten years. Hepatitis B, like the HIV virus, can be passed on through unprotected sexual contact, blood transfusions and dirty needles. The very effective vaccine (three injections over six months) is recommended for anyone in a high-risk category, including those travelling extensively in rural areas for prolonged periods, with access to only basic medical care. It's also now possible – and cheaper – to have a combined vaccination against both hepatitis A and B: the course comprises three injections over six months.

The risks of contracting Japanese encephalitis are extremely small, but, as the disease is untreatable, those travelling for a month or more in the countryside, especially in the north during and soon after the summer rainy season (June–Nov), should consider immunization. The course consists of two or three injections over a month with the last dose administered at least ten days before departure. Note that it is not recommended for those with liver, heart or kidney disorders, or for multiple-allergy sufferers. If your plans include long stays in remote areas your doctor may also recommend vaccination against meningitis (a single shot) and rabies.

Mosquito-borne diseases

Both the Red River and Mekong deltas (including Hanoi and Ho Chi Minh City) have few incidences of malaria. The coastal plain north of Nha Trang is also considered relatively safe. Malaria occurs frequently in the highlands and rural areas, notably the central highlands, as well as the southern provinces of Ca Mau, Bac Lieu and Tay Ninh. The majority of cases involve the most dangerous strain, Plasmodium falciparum, which can be fatal if not treated promptly.

The key preventive measure is to avoid getting bitten by mosquitoes (which carry the disease), but if you're travelling in high-risk areas it's advisable to take preventive tablets.

Mosquitoes are also responsible for transmitting dengue fever and Japanese encephalitis. Dengue is carried by a variety of mosquitoes active in the daytime (particularly two hours after sunrise and several hours before sunset) and occurs mostly in the Mekong Delta, including Ho Chi Minh City, though the chances of being infected remain small. There is a more dangerous version called dengue hemorrhage fever, which primarily affects children but is extremely rare among foreign visitors to Vietnam. If you notice an unusual tendency to bleed or bruise, seek medical advice immediately.

There are several things you can do to avoid getting bitten. Mosquitoes are most active at dawn and dusk, so at these times wear long sleeves, trousers and socks, avoid dark colors and perfumes, which attract mosquitoes, and put repellent on all exposed skin. Sprays and lotions containing around thirty to forty percent DEET (diethyltoluamide) are effective and can also be used to treat clothes, but the chemical is toxic: keep it away from eyes and open wounds.

Many hotels and guesthouses provide mosquito nets over beds or meshing on windows and doors. Air-conditioning and fans also help keep mosquitoes at bay, as do mosquito coils and knockdown insecticide sprays (available locally), though none of these measures is as effective as a decent net.

Bites and creepy-crawlies

Bed bugs, fleas, lice or scabies can be picked up from dirty bedclothes, though this is relatively unusual in Vietnam. Try not to scratch bites, which easily become septic. Ticks picked up walking through scrub may carry a strain of typhus; carry out regular body inspections and remove ticks promptly.

Rabies is contracted by being bitten, or even licked on broken skin or the eyes, by an infected animal. The best strategy is to give all animals, especially dogs, cats and monkeys, a wide berth.

Vietnam has several poisonous snakes but in general, snakes steer clear of humans and it's very rare to get bitten. Avoid walking through long grass or undergrowth, and wear boots when walking off-road. If bitten, immobilize the limb (most snake bites occur on the lower leg) to slow down absorption of the venom and remove any tight-fitting socks or other clothing from around the wound. It's important to seek medical assistance as quickly as possible. It helps if you can take the (dead) snake to be identified, or at least remember what it looked like.

Leeches are more common and, though harmless, can be unpleasant. Long trousers, sleeves and socks help prevent them getting a grip. The best way to get rid of leeches is to burn them off with a lighted match or cigarette; alternatively rub alcohol or salt onto them.

Worms enter the body either via contaminated food, or through the skin, especially the soles of the feet. You may notice worms in your stools, or experience other indications such as mild abdominal pain leading, very rarely, to acute intestinal blockage (roundworm, the most common), an itchy anus (threadworm) or anaemia (hookworm).

An infestation is easily treated with worming tablets from a pharmacy.

Heat trouble

Don't underestimate the strength of the tropical sun: sunburn can be avoided by restricting your exposure to the midday sun and liberal use of high-factor sunscreens. Drinking plenty of water will prevent dehydration, but if you do become dehydrated – signs are infrequent or irregular urination – drink a salt and sugar solution.

Heatstroke is more serious and may require hospital treatment. Indications are a high temperature, lack of sweating, a fast pulse and red skin. Reducing your body temperature with a lukewarm shower will provide initial relief.

High humidity often causes heat rashes, prickly heat and fungal infections. Prevention and cure are the same: wear loose clothes made of natural fibers, wash frequently and dry off thoroughly afterwards. Talcum powder helps, particularly zinc oxide-based products (prickly heat powder), as does the use of mild antiseptic soap.

Sexually transmitted diseases

Until recently Vietnam carried out very little screening for sex workers, injecting drug users and other high-risk groups. As a result, sexually transmitted diseases such as gonorrhea, syphilis and AIDS had been flourishing, though fortunately awareness is growing and the number of AIDS victims, at least, is levelling out. It is, therefore, extremely unwise to contemplate casual unprotected sex, and bear in mind that Vietnamese condoms (bao cao su) are often poor-quality (more reliable imported varieties are available in major cities).

Getting medical help

Pharmacies can generally help with minor injuries or ailments and in major towns you will usually find a pharmacist who speaks English.

The selection of reliable Asian and Western products on the market is improving rapidly, and both Ho Chi Minh City and Hanoi now have well-stocked pharmacies. That said, drugs past their shelf life and even counterfeit medicines are rife, so inspect packaging carefully, check use-by dates – and bring anything you know you're likely to need from home, including oral contraceptives. Tampons and reliable, imported brands of condoms (bao cao su) are sold in Hanoi and Ho Chi Minh, but don't count on getting them easily elsewhere.

Local hospitals can also treat minor problems, but in a real emergency your best bet is to head for Hanoi or Ho Chi Minh City. Hospitals in both these cities can handle most eventualities and you also have the option of one of the excellent international medical centres. Note that doctors and hospitals expect immediate cash payment for health services rendered; you will then have to seek reimbursement from your insurance company (make sure you get receipts for any payments you make).

The media

Vietnam has several English–language newspapers and magazines, of which the daily Viet Nam News (vietnamnews.vnagency.com.vn) has the widest distribution. It provides a brief – and very select – run–down of local, regional and international news, as well as snippets on art and culture. Though short on general news, both the weekly Vietnam Investment Review (wvir.com.vn) and the monthly Vietnam Economic Times (vneconomy.vn) cover issues in greater depth and are worth looking at for an insight into what makes the Vietnamese economy tick. Both also publish useful supplements (Time Out and The Guide respectively) with selective but up–to–date restaurant and nightlife listings mainly covering Hanoi and Ho Chi Minh City, plus feature articles on culture and tourist destinations. However, they have been superseded by the excellent free magazines The Word and AsiaLife, which both carry listings of bars and restaurants as well as articles on aspects of Vietnamese culture; look out for them in establishments that advertise in these publications.

All media in Vietnam are under tight government control. There is, however, a slight glimmer of less draconian censorship, with an increasing number of stories covering corruption at even quite senior levels and more criticism of government policies and ministers, albeit very mild by Western standards.

Foreign publications, such as the International Herald Tribune, Time, Newsweek, The Financial Times and the Bangkok Post are sold by street vendors and at some of the larger bookshops and in the newsstands of more upmarket hotels in Ho Chi Minh City and Hanoi.

The government radio station, Voice of Vietnam (english.vov.vn), began life in 1945 during the August Revolution. It became famous during the American War when "Hanoi Hannah" broadcast propaganda programs to American GIs. Nowadays it maintains six channels, of which VOV5 broadcasts English-language programs several times a day covering a whole range of subjects: news, weather, sport, entertainment and culture, even market prices. You can pick up the broadcasts on FM in and around Hanoi and Ho Chi Minh City.

To keep in touch with the full spectrum of international news, however, you'll need to go online or get a short-wave radio to pick up one of the world service channels, such as BBC World Service (wbbc.co.uk/worldservice), Radio Canada International (wrcinet.ca) and Voice of America (wvoanews.com); local frequencies are listed on the relevant website.

Vietnamese television (VTV, wvtv.gov.vn) is also government-run and airs a mix of films, music shows, news programs, soaps, sport and foreign (mostly American, Korean and Japanese) imports. VTV1, the main domestic channel, occasionally presents a news summary in English. However, most hotels provide satellite TV, offering BBC, CNN, MTV and HBO as standard.

Crime and personal safety

Vietnam is a relatively safe country for visitors, including women travelling alone. In fact, given the country's recent history, many tourists, particularly Americans, are pleasantly surprised at the warm reception that foreign travelers receive. That said, petty crime is on the rise – though it's still relatively small–scale and shouldn't be a problem if you take common–sense precautions. Generally, the hassles you'll encounter will be the milder sort of coping with pushy vendors and over–enthusiastic touts and beggars.

Petty crime

As a tourist, you're an obvious target for thieves (who may include your fellow travelers): carry your passport, travelers' cheques and other valuables in a concealed money belt. Don't leave anything important lying about in your room: use a safe, if you have one. A cable lock, or padlock and chain, comes in handy for doors and windows in cheap hotels, and is useful for securing your pack on trains and buses. It's not a bad idea to keep $100 or so separate from the rest of your cash, along with insurance policy details and photocopies of important documents, such as the relevant pages of your passport including your visa stamp.

At street level it's best not to be ostentatious: forego eye-catching jewelry and flashy watches, try to be discreet when taking out your cash, and be particularly wary in crowds and on public transport. If your pack is on the top of the bus, make sure it's attached securely (usually everything is tied down with ropes) and keep an eye on it during the most vulnerable times – before departure, at meal stops and on arrival at your destination. On trains, either cable-lock your pack or put it under the bottom bench-seat, out of public view. The odd instance has been reported of travelers being drugged and then robbed, so it's best not to accept food or drink from anyone you don't know and trust. Bear in mind that when walking or riding in a cyclo you are vulnerable to moped-borne snatch-thieves; don't wear cameras or expensive sunglasses hanging around your neck and keep a firm grip on your bags. If you do become a target, however, it's best to let go rather than risk being pulled into the traffic and suffering serious injury.

The place you are most likely to encounter street crime is in Ho Chi Minh City, which has a fairly bad reputation for bag-snatchers, pickpockets and con artists. Be wary of innocent-looking kids and grannies who may be acting as decoys for thieves – especially in the bar districts and other popular tourist hangouts. It's best to avoid taking a cyclo at night, and you'd be unwise to walk alone at any time outside Districts One and Three.

Petty crime, much of it drug- and prostitution-related, is also a problem in Nha Trang, where you should watch your belongings at all times on the beach. Again, be wary of taking a cyclo after dark and women should avoid walking alone at night. Single males, on the other hand, are a particular target for "taxi girls", many of whom also double as thieves.

It's important not to get paranoid, however: crime levels in Vietnam are still a long way behind those of Western countries, and violent crime against tourists is extremely rare.

If you do have anything stolen, you'll need to go to the nearest police station to make a report in order to claim on your insurance. Try to recruit an English-speaker to come along with you – someone at your hotel should be able to help.

"Social Evils" and serious crime

Since liberalization and doi moi, Vietnamese society has seen an increase in prostitution, drugs – including hard drugs – and more serious crimes. These so-called "social evils" are viewed as a direct consequence of reduced controls on society and ensuing Westernization. The police have imposed midnight closing on bars and clubs for several years now, mainly because of drugs, but also to curb general rowdiness, although you'll always find the occasional bar that somehow manages to keep serving, particularly around De Tham in Ho Chi Minh City. That apart, the campaign against social evils should have little effect on most foreign tourists.

Single Western males tend to get solicited by prostitutes in cheap provincial and seaside hotels, though more commonly by women cruising on motorbikes. Quite apart from any higher moral considerations, bear in mind that AIDS is a serious problem in Vietnam, though the epidemic has shown signs of stabilizing.

Finally, having anything to do with drugs in Vietnam is extremely unwise. At night there's a fair amount of drug selling on the streets of Ho Chi Minh City, Hanoi, Nha Trang and even Sa Pa, and it's not unknown for dealers to turn buyers in to the police. Fines and jail sentences are imposed for lesser offences, while the death penalty is regularly imposed for possessing, trading or smuggling larger quantities.

Military and political hazards

Not surprisingly, the Vietnamese authorities are sensitive about military installations and strategic areas – including border regions, military camps (of which there are many), bridges, airports, naval dockyards and even train stations. Anyone taking photographs in the vicinity of such sites risks having the memory card removed from their camera or being fined.

Unexploded ordnance from past conflicts still poses a threat in some areas: the problem is most acute in the Demilitarized Zone, where each year a number of local farmers, scrap-metal scavengers or children are killed or injured. Wherever you are, stick to well-trodden paths and never touch any shells or half-buried chunks of metal.

Beggars, hassle and scams

Given the number of disabled, war-wounded and unemployed in Vietnam, there are surprisingly few beggars around. Most people are actually trying hard to earn a living somehow, and many day-tours include a visit to a factory that employs disabled workers to produce handicrafts or local products.

At many tourist spots, you may well be swamped by a gaggle of children or teenagers selling cold drinks, fruit and chewing gum. Although they can sometimes be a bit overwhelming, as often as not they're just out to practice their English and be entertained for a while. They may even turn out to be excellent guides, in which case it's only fair that you buy something from them in return.

A common scam among taxi drivers is to tell new arrivals in a town that the hotel they ask for is closed or has moved or changed its name. Instead, they head for a hotel that pays them commission. This may work out fine (new hotels often use this method to become known), but more often than not it's a substandard hotel and you will in any case pay over the odds since the room rate will include the driver's commission. To avoid being ripped off, always insist on being taken to the exact address of your chosen hotel, at least just to check the story.

Another common complaint is that organized tours don't live up to what was promised. There are more people on the tour than stated, for example, or the room doesn't have air-conditioning, or the guide's English is limited. If it's a group tour and you've paid up front, unfortunately there's very little you can do beyond complaining to the agent on your return; you may be lucky and get some form of compensation, but it's very unlikely. As always, you tend to get what you pay for, so avoid signing up for dirt-cheap tours.

Women travelers

Vietnam is generally a safe country for women to travel around alone. Most Vietnamese will simply be curious as to why you are on your own and the chances of encountering any threatening behaviour are extremely rare. That said, it pays to take the normal precautions, especially late at night when there are few people on the streets and

you should avoid taking a cyclo by yourself; use a taxi instead –
metered taxis are generally considered safest.

Most Vietnamese women dress modestly, keeping covered from top
to toe, unless their profession requires them to show off their assets. It
helps to dress modestly too and to avoid wearing skimpy shorts and
vests, which are considered by some men an invitation to paid sex.
Topless sunbathing, even beside a hotel pool, is a complete no-no.

Festivals and religious events

The Vietnamese year follows a rhythm of festivals and religious observances, ranging from solemn family gatherings at the ancestral altar to national celebrations culminating in Tet, the Vietnamese New Year. In between are countless local festivals, most notably in the Red River Delta, honoring the tutelary spirit of the village or community temple.

The majority of festivals take place in spring, with a second flurry in the autumn months. One festival you might want to make a note of, however, is Tet: not only does most of Vietnam close down for the week, but either side of the holiday local transport services are stretched to the limit and international flights are filled by returning overseas Vietnamese.

Many Vietnamese festivals are Chinese in origin, imbued with a distinctive flavor over the centuries, but minority groups also hold their own specific celebrations. The ethnic minorities continue to punctuate the year with rituals that govern sowing, harvest or hunting, as well as elaborate rites of passage surrounding birth and death. The Cao Dai religion has its own array of festivals, while Christian communities throughout Vietnam observe the major ceremonies. Christmas is marked as a religious ceremony only by the faithful, though it's becoming a major event for all Vietnamese as an excuse to shop and party, with sax-playing Santas greeting shoppers in front of malls.

The ceremonies you're most likely to see are weddings and funerals. The tenth lunar month is the most auspicious time for weddings, though at other times you'll also encounter plenty of wedding cavalcades on the road, their lead vehicle draped in colorful ribbons. Funeral processions are recognizable from the white headbands worn by mourners, while close family members dress completely in white. Both weddings and funerals are characterized by street side parties under makeshift marquees, and since both tend to be joyous occasions, it's often difficult to know what you're witnessing, unless you spot a bridal gown or portrait of the deceased on display.

Most festivals take place according to the lunar calendar, which is also closely linked to the Chinese system with a zodiac of twelve animal signs. The most important times during the lunar month (which lasts 29 or 30 days) are the full moon (day one) and the new moon (day fourteen or fifteen). Festivals are often held at these times, which also hold a special significance for Buddhists, who are supposed to pray at the pagoda and avoid eating meat during the two days. On the eve of each full moon, Hoi An now celebrates a Full-Moon Festival: traffic is barred from the town center, where traditional games, dance and music performances take place under the light of silk lanterns.

All Vietnamese calendars show both the lunar and solar (Gregorian) months and dates, but to be sure of a festival date it's best to check locally.

Tết: The Vietnamese New Year

"Tet", simply meaning festival, is the accepted name for Vietnam's most important annual event, properly known as Tet Nguyen Dan, or festival of the first day. Tet lasts for seven days and falls sometime between the last week of January and the third week of February, on the night of the new moon. This is a time when families get together to celebrate renewal and hope for the new year, when ancestral spirits are welcomed back to the household and when everyone in Vietnam becomes a year older – age is reckoned by the new year and not by individual birthdays.

There's an almost tangible sense of excitement leading up to midnight on the eve of Tet, though the welcoming of the new year is now a much more subdued – and less dangerous – affair since firecrackers were banned in 1995. Instead, all the major cities hold fireworks displays.

Tet kicks off seven days before the new moon with the festival of Ong Tau, the god of the hearth (23rd day of the twelfth month). Ong Tau keeps watch over the household throughout the year, wards off evil spirits and makes an annual report of family events, good or bad, to the Jade Emperor. In order to send Ong Tau off to heaven in a benevolent mood, the family cleans its house from top to bottom, and makes offerings to him, including pocket money and a new set of clothes. Ong Tau returns home at midnight on the first chime of the new year and it's this, together with welcoming the ancestral spirits back to share in the party, that warrants such a massive celebration.

Tet is all about starting the year afresh, with a clean slate and good intentions. Not only is the house scrubbed, but all debts are paid off and those who can afford it have a haircut and buy new clothes. To attract favorable spirits, good-luck charms are put in the house, most commonly cockerels or the trinity of male figures representing prosperity, happiness and longevity. The crucial moments are the first minutes and hours of the new year as these set the pattern for the whole of the following year. People strive to avoid arguments, swearing or breaking anything – at least during the first three days when a single ill word could tempt bad luck into the house for the whole year ahead. The first visitor on the morning of Tet is also vitally significant: the ideal is someone respected, wealthy and happily married who will bring good fortune to the family; the bereaved, unemployed, accident-prone and even pregnant, on the other hand, are considered ill-favored. This honor carries with it an onerous responsibility, however: if the family has a bad year, it will be the first-footer's fault.

The week-long festival is marked by feasting: special foods are eaten at Tet, such as pickled vegetables, candied lotus seeds and sugared fruits, all of which are first offered at the family altar. The most famous delicacy is banh chung (banh tet in the south), a thick square or cylinder of sweet, sticky rice that is prepared only for Tet. The rice is wrapped around a mixture of green-bean paste, pork fat and meat marinated in nuoc mam, and then boiled in banana leaves, which impart a pale green colour. According to legend, an impoverished prince of the Hung dynasty invented the cakes over two thousand years ago; his father was so impressed by the simplicity of his son's gift that he named the prince as his heir. Tet is an expensive time for Vietnamese families, many of whom save for months to get the new year off to a good start. Apart from special foods and new clothes, it's traditional to give children red envelopes containing li xi, or lucky money, and to decorate homes with spring blossoms. In the week before Tet, flower markets grace the larger cities: peach blossoms in the north, apricot in Hué and mandarin in the south. Plum and kumquat (symbolizing gold coins) are also popular, alongside the more showy, modern blooms of roses, dahlias or gladioli.

Sports & Activities

Though Vietnam was slow to develop its huge potential as an outdoor adventure destination, things have really changed in the last few years. Apart from trekking in the mountainous north, visitors can now also go rock–climbing, canyoning, sea kayaking or kitesurfing, among other activities. Da Lat has emerged as Vietnam's adventure sports capital and Mui Ne its surf city, though some sports like mountain biking can be done throughout the country.

Trekking

The easiest and most popular area for trekking is in the northwest mountains around Sa Pa and, to a lesser extent, Mai Chau. Sa Pa is also the starting point for ascents of the country's highest peak, Fan Si Pan, a challenge to be undertaken only by experienced hikers. Other options include hiking around Kon Tum or Da Lat in the central highlands or in one of Vietnam's many national parks, including Cat Ba, Cuc Phuong, Bach Ma, Cat Tien and Yok Don. In Yok Don you can even go elephant trekking, though prices are rather steep.

There's no problem about striking out on your own for a day's hiking. However, for anything more adventurous, particularly if you want to overnight in the villages, you'll need to make arrangements in advance. This is easily done either before you arrive in Vietnam or through local tour agents, most of which offer organized tours and tailor-made packages. In most cases you can also make arrangements through guesthouses and guides on the spot. Note that it's essential to take a guide if you are keen to get off the beaten track: many areas are still sensitive about the presence of foreigners.

Biking

Mountain biking is becoming increasingly popular in Vietnam. The classic ride is from Hanoi to Ho Chi Minh City, a journey of between two and three weeks. Previously, this would have taken you along Highway 1, battling with trucks and buses, but now the more switched-on tour companies are offering excursions down the Ho Chi

Minh Highway which runs along the western Truong Son mountain chain, and is so far thankfully free of heavy traffic.

The area around Sa Pa is a focus for biking activity, with tour operators offering excursions to suit all levels of experience and fitness. You can choose from half-day excursions to multi-day outings including overnighting in minority villages. Other good areas for exploring by bike include Mai Chau, Bac Ha, Da Lat and the Mekong Delta.

North Vietnam is also popular among the motor biking fraternity. Specialist outfits in Hanoi organize tailor-made itineraries taking you way off the beaten track.

Watersports

With its three-thousand-kilometer coastline, Vietnam should be a paradise for watersports, but the options remain fairly limited at present, for a variety of reasons. One is simply a matter of access: the infrastructure is not yet in place. More crucial is the presence of potentially dangerous undercurrents along much of the coast, accompanied by strong winds at certain times of year. Many of the big beach resorts have guards or put out flags in season indicating where it's safe to swim. Elsewhere, check carefully before taking the plunge.

Whilst many of the beaches along the coast are great for swimming, the best are those around Mui Ne and Nha Trang, with Hoi An and Da Nang close behind. Mui Ne is also the country's top venue for windsurfing and kitesurfing, both of which are now hugely popular. Phu Quoc Island, off Vietnam's southern coast, is also famed not only for its fabulous beaches but also as the country's top spot for snorkeling and scuba-diving. The Con Dao Islands and Nha Trang are other popular places to don a snorkel or wet suit, but wherever you dive, it's worth noting that standards of maintenance aren't always great, so check equipment carefully and only go out with a properly qualified and registered operator that you trust.

Heading inland, the rivers and waterfalls around Da Lat provide good possibilities for canyoning and rock-climbing, though Cat Ba Island is a good alternative if you'd like to combine rock-climbing with sightseeing in Ha Long Bay.

Mui Ne has a good reputation for windsurfing and kitesurfing, and even hosts an international competition in these sports each spring (usually Feb).

In north Vietnam Ha Long Bay is the water sports center, while rock-climbing is becoming big as well, organized from Cat Ba. Most boat tours of the bay allow time for swimming – weather permitting – while there are decent beaches on Cat Ba and better still on remote Quan Lan Island. For those in search of more strenuous exercise, a number of tour agents offer sea-kayaking trips on the bay – not recommended in the heat of summer.

Other activities

Vietnam has over 850 species of birds, including several that have only been identified in the past few years. The best places for birdwatching are the national parks, including Cuc Phuong (famous also for its springtime butterfly displays), Bach Ma and Cat Tien. The rare Sarus crane, amongst many other species, spends the dry season in and around the Tram Chim National Park in the Mekong Delta. For more information, check out vietnambirding.com or birdwatchingvietnam.net.

Finally, there are now dozens of excellent golf courses in Vietnam – around Ho Chi Minh City, Hanoi, Phan Thiet and Da Lat amongst others – all with much cheaper green fees than in the West.

Shopping

Souvenir–hunters will find rich pickings in Vietnam, whose eye–catching handicrafts and mementos range from colonial currency and stamps to fabrics and basket ware crafted by the country's ethnic minorities, and from limpet–like conical hats to fake US Army–issue Zippo lighters. Throughout the Guide, I've highlighted places to shop, but in general you'll find the best quality, choice and prices in Ho Chi Minh City, Hanoi and Hoi An. Though you'll find more shops now have fixed prices, particularly those catering to tourists, in markets and rural areas prices are almost always open to negotiation.

Clothing, arts and crafts

Few Western tourists leave Vietnam without the obligatory conical hat, or non la, sewn from rain- and sun-proof palm fronds; at around 25,000đ for a basic version, they're definitely an affordable keepsake.

From the city of Hué comes a more elaborate version, the poem hat, or non bai tho, in whose brim are inlays which, when held up to the light, reveal lines of poetry or scenes from Vietnamese legend. Vietnamese women traditionally wear the ao dai – baggy silk trousers under a knee-length silk tunic slit up both sides. Extraordinarily elegant, ao dai can be bought off the peg anywhere in the country for around $30; or, if you can spare a few days for fitting, you can have one tailor-made for $40 or so, depending on the material.

Local silk is sold by the meter in Vietnam's more sizeable markets and in countless outlets in Hoi An, along Dong Khoi in Ho Chi Minh City and on Hanoi's Hang Gai. These same shops also sell ready-made clothes and accessories, including embroidered silk handbags and shoes, and most also offer tailoring. In general, Hoi An's tailors have the best reputation, either working from a pattern book or copying an item you take along. Just make sure you allow plenty of time for fittings.

Embroidered cotton, in the form of tablecloths, sheets and pillowcases, also makes a popular souvenir. Meanwhile, the sartorial needs of backpackers are well catered for in major tourist destinations, where T-shirt sellers do brisk business. Predictably popular designs include a portrait of Uncle Ho, and the yellow Communist star on a red background.

Traditional handicrafts

Of the many types of traditional handicrafts on offer in Vietnam, lacquerware (son mai) is among the most beautiful. It is also incredibly light, so won't add significantly to your baggage weight. Made by applying multiple layers of resin onto an article and then polishing vigorously to achieve a deep, lustrous sheen, lacquer is used to decorate furniture, boxes, chopsticks and bangles and is sometimes embellished with eggshell or inlays of mother-of-pearl (which is also used in its own right, on screens and pictures) – common motifs are animals, fish and elaborate scrolling. More recently, the lacquerware tradition has been hijacked by more contemporary icons, and it's now possible to buy colorful lacquerware paintings of Mickey Mouse, Tin Tin and Batman. Imported synthetic lacquer has also made an appearance. These brightly colored, almost metallic, finishes may not be for the purist, but they make for eye-catching bowls, vases and all sorts of household items.

Bronze, brass and jade are also put to good use, appearing in various forms such as carvings, figurines and jewelry. In Hué, brass and copper teapots are popular. Of the porcelain and ceramics available across the country, thigh-high ceramic elephants and other animal figurines are the quirkiest buys – though decidedly tricky to carry home. Look out, too, for boxes and other knick-knacks made from wonderfully aromatic cinnamon and camphor wood. For something a little more culturally elevated, you could invest in a water-puppet or a traditional musical instrument.

Vietnam's ethnic minorities are producing increasingly sophisticated fare for the tourist market. Fabrics – sometimes shot through with shimmering gold braid – are their main asset, sold in lengths and also made into purses, shoulder bags and other accoutrements. The minorities of the central highlands are adept at basketwork, fashioning backpacks, baskets and mats, and bamboo pipes. Hanoi probably has the greatest variety of minority handicrafts on sale, though you'll also find plenty available in Ho Chi Minh City. In the far north, Sa Pa is a popular place to buy Hmong clothes, bags and skull-caps, and you'll find lengths of woven fabrics or embroidery in markets throughout the northern mountains.

Paintings

A healthy fine arts scene exists in Vietnam, and painting in particular is thriving. In the galleries of Hanoi, Ho Chi Minh City and Hoi An you'll find exquisite works in oil, watercolor, lacquer, charcoal and silk weaving by the country's leading artists. Hanoi is the best single place to look for contemporary art.

For the top names you can expect to pay hundreds or even thousands of dollars. Buyer beware, however: many artists find it lucrative to knock out multiple copies of their own or other people's work. You'll need to know what you're doing, or to buy from a reputable gallery.

A cheap alternative is to snap up a reproduction of a famous image by Dali or Van Gogh, while something essentially Vietnamese are the Communist propaganda posters, which are on sale everywhere.

Books, stamps and coins

You can buy photocopied editions of almost all the books ever published on Vietnam from strolling vendors in Hanoi and Ho Chi Minh City. There are also an increasing number of locally published coffee-table books, histories and guides available from bona-fide bookshops and the more upmarket hotels. However, if all you want is some general reading matter, both Hanoi and Ho Chi Minh City now have secondhand bookshops where you can exchange or buy used books.

Philatelists meanwhile will enjoy browsing through the old Indochinese stamps sold in the souvenir shops

of Hanoi and Ho Chi Minh City. Similarly, old notes and coins, including French-issue piastres and US Army credits, are available.

Memorabilia, trinkets and food

Army surplus gear is still a money-spinner, though fatigues, belts, canteens and dog tags purportedly stolen from a dead or wounded GI aren't the most tasteful of souvenirs – and the vast majority are fakes anyway. The green pith helmets with a red star on the front, worn first by the NVA during the American War and now by the regular Vietnamese Army, find more takers. Other items that sell like hot cakes, especially in the south, are fake Zippo lighters bearing such pithy adages as "When I die bury me face down, so the whole damn army can kiss my ass" and "We are the unwilling, led by the unqualified, doin' the unnecessary for the ungrateful", though again they're very unlikely to be authentic GI issue. In Ho Chi Minh City, extravagant wooden model ships are sold in a string of shops on Hai Ba Trung, at the east side of Lam Son Square.

Finally, foodstuffs that may tempt you include coffee from the central highlands, candied strawberries and artichoke tea from Da Lat, coconut candies from the Mekong Delta, preserved miniature tangerines from Hoi An and packets of tea and dried herbs and spices from the northern highlands. As for drinks, most of the concoctions itemized in A Traditional Tipple are securely bottled. The Soc Tinh range of rice-distilled liquor makes an attractively packaged souvenir.

Essentials

Addresses

Locating an address is rarely a problem in Vietnam, but there are a couple of conventions it helps to know about. Where two numbers are separated by a slash, such as 110 5, you simply make for no. 110, where an alley will lead off to a further batch of buildings – you want the fifth one. Where a number is followed by a letter, as in 117a, you're looking for a single block encompassing several addresses, of which one will be 117a. Vietnamese cite addresses without the words for street, avenue and so on; I've followed this practice throughout the Guide except where ambiguity would result.

Admission charges

Admission charges are usually levied at museums, historic sights, national parks and any place that attracts tourists – sometimes even beaches. Charges at some major sights range from a dollar or two up to around US$4–5 for the Cham ruins at My Son or Hué's citadel and royal mausoleums. Elsewhere, however, the amount is usually just a few thousand dong. Note that there's often a hefty additional fee for cameras and videos at major sights.

Apart from those with some historical significance, pagodas and temples are usually free, though it's customary to leave a donation of a few thousand dong in the collecting box or on one of the altar plates.

Costs

With the average Vietnamese annual income hovering around US$800–1000, daily expenses are low, and if you come prepared to do as the locals do, then food and drink can be incredibly cheap – and even accommodation needn't be too great an expense. However, constantly rising petrol prices mean that transport costs are creeping up all the time. Bargaining is very much a part of everyday life, and almost everything is negotiable, from fruit in the market to a room for the night.

By eating at simple com (rice) and pho (noodle soup) stalls, picking up local buses and opting for the simplest accommodation there's no reason why you shouldn't be able to adhere to a daily budget in the region of US$15–20. Upgrading to more salubrious lodgings with a few mod cons, eating good food followed by a couple of beers in a bar and signing up for the odd minibus tour and visiting a few sights could bounce your expenditure up to a more realistic US$30–40. A fair mid-level budget, treating yourself to three-star hotels and more upmarket restaurants, would lie in the US$50–100 range, depending on the number and type of tours you took. And if you stay at the ritziest city hotels, dine at the swankiest restaurants and rent cars with drivers wherever you go, then the sky's the limit.

Electricity

The electricity supply in Vietnam is 220 volts. Plugs generally have two round pins, though you may come across sockets requiring two flat pins and even some requiring three pins. Adaptors can be found in any electrical shop. Power supplies can be erratic, so be prepared for cuts and surges.

Entry requirements

All foreign nationals need a visa to enter Vietnam, with certain exceptions: citizens of Sweden, Denmark, Norway, Finland, Japan and South Korea do not need a visa if they are travelling to Vietnam for less than fifteen days, have a passport valid for three months following the date of entry and hold a return air ticket. Citizens of certain ASEAN–member countries, including Thailand, Malaysia and Singapore are also exempt for stays of up to thirty days. Tourist visas are generally valid for thirty days and for a single entry, though three months multiple–entry visas are also available. A standard thirty–day visa costs the local equivalent of US$30–100, depending on how quickly you want it processed.

The majority of visitors apply for a visa in their country of residence, either from the embassy direct, or through a specialist visa agent or tour agent. Processing normally takes around a week, though many embassies also offer a more expensive "express" service.

If it's difficult to get to your nearest Vietnam Embassy, consider buying your visa online at wvietnamvisa.com. Prices range from US$22 plus US$25 'stamping fee' (for a one-month, single-entry visa) to US$34 plus US$50 'stamping fee' (for a three-month, multiple-entry visa.) On receipt of your fee (usually within 24 hours), you'll be sent a document to print out and show immigration on arrival. The process is very efficient and currently only requires a short wait upon arrival, though this wait could get longer if the system proves popular. If you follow this route, look out for the Visa on Arrival desk at the airport before you pass through immigration.

To apply for a tourist visa, you have to submit an application form with one or two passport-sized photographs (procedures vary) and the fee. The visa shows specific start and end dates indicating the period of validity within which you can enter and leave the country. The visa is valid for entry via Hanoi, Ho Chi Minh City and Da Nang international airports and any of Vietnam's land borders open to foreigners.

Business visas are valid for one month upwards and can be issued for multiple entry, though you'll need a sponsoring office in Vietnam to underwrite your application.

One-year student visas are relatively easy to get hold of if you enroll, for example, on a Vietnamese language course at one of the universities; you'll be required to attend a minimum number of classes per week to qualify. It's easiest to arrange it in advance, but you can enter Vietnam on a tourist visa and apply for student status later – the only downside is that you may have to leave the country in order to get the visa stamp.

Special circumstances affect overseas Vietnamese holding a foreign passport: check with the Vietnamese embassy in your country of residence for details.

Visa extensions

Thirty-day extensions are issued in Hanoi, Ho Chi Minh City, Nha Trang, Da Nang, Hué and Hoi An. Some people have managed to obtain second and even third extensions, usually in Hanoi and Ho Chi Minh City. Applications have to be made via a tour agent. In general, they take three to five days to process and cost $25 for the first one-month extension.

Holders of business visas can apply for an extension only through the office that sponsored their original visa, backed up with reasons as to why an extension is necessary.

Incidentally, overstaying your visa will result in fines of between US$10 and US$50, depending how long you overstay and the mood of the immigration official, and is not recommended.

Culture and etiquette

With its blend of Confucianism and Buddhism, Vietnamese society tends to be both conservative and, at the same time, fairly tolerant. This means you will rarely be remonstrated with for your dress or behaviour, even if your hosts do disapprove. By following a few simple rules, you can minimize the risk of causing offence. This is particularly important in rural areas and small towns where people are less used to the eccentric habits of foreigners.

As a visitor, it's recommended that you err on the side of caution. Shorts and sleeveless shirts are fine for the beach, but are not welcome in pagodas, temples and other religious sites. When dealing with officialdom, it also pays to look as neat and tidy as possible. Anything else may be taken as a mark of disrespect.

Women in particular should dress modestly, especially in the countryside and ethnic minority areas, where revealing too much flesh is regarded as offensive.

It's also worth noting that nudity, either male or female, on the beach is absolutely beyond the pale.

When entering a Cao Dai temple, the main building of a pagoda or a private home it's the custom to remove your shoes. In some pagodas nowadays this may only be required when stepping onto the prayer mats – ask or watch what other people do. In a pagoda or temple, you are also expected to leave a small donation.

Officially, homosexuality is regarded as a "social evil", alongside drugs and prostitution. However, there is no law explicitly banning homosexual activity and, as long as it is not practiced openly, it is largely ignored. Indeed, the number of openly gay men has increased noticeably in recent years, particularly in Ho Chi Minh City and Hanoi, and homosexuality is discussed more frequently in the media, although the lesbian scene remains very low-key. Although outward discrimination is rare, this is still a very traditional society and it pays to be discreet in Vietnam. For more information, consult the excellent Utopia Asia website, utopia-asia.com.

As in most Asian countries, it's not done to get angry, and it certainly won't get things moving any quicker. Passing round cigarettes (to men only) is always appreciated and is widely used as a social gambit aimed at progressing tricky negotiations, bargaining and so forth.

Tipping, while not expected, is always appreciated. In general, a few thousand dong should suffice. Smart restaurants and hotels normally add a service charge, but if not ten percent is the norm in a restaurant, while the amount in a hotel will depend on the grade of hotel and what services they've provided. If you're pleased with the service, you should also tip the guide, and the driver where appropriate, at the end of a tour.

Other social conventions worth noting are that you shouldn't touch children on the head and, unlike in the West, it's best to ignore a young baby rather than praise it, since it's believed that this attracts the attention of jealous spirits who will cause the baby to fall ill.

Insurance

It is essential to have a good travel insurance policy to cover against theft, loss and illness or injury. It's also advisable to have medical cover that includes evacuation in the event of serious illness, as the local hospitals aren't that great. Most policies exclude so-called dangerous sports unless an extra premium is paid: in Vietnam this can include scuba diving, whitewater rafting, kite surfing, rock climbing and trekking. If you're doing any motorbike touring, you are strongly advised to take out full medical insurance including emergency evacuation; make sure the policy specifically covers you for biking in Vietnam, and ascertain whether benefits will be paid as treatment proceeds or only after return home, and whether there is a 24-hour medical emergency number. If you need to make a claim, you should keep receipts for medicines and medical treatment, and in the event that you have anything stolen, you must obtain an official statement from the police.

Internet and email

Accessing the internet in Vietnam has become a great deal easier, though it is still monitored and controlled by a government fearful of this potentially subversive means of communication. Occasionally social networking sites like Facebook have been blocked.

There's no problem about logging on in the major cities and tourist centres in Vietnam, where you'll find dozens of internet cafés, while many hotels also offer internet access. Many upmarket and even some budget hotels offer Wi-Fi broadband access in your room – sometimes free to attract custom. Even remote regions are wired to the web these days, though the service may be slower and more expensive. Rates in the big cities currently stand at around 100đ per minute, with some places charging by the hour (about 6000đ).

Laundry

Most top- and mid-range hotels provide a laundry service, and many budget hotels too, but rates can vary wildly, so it's worth checking first. In the bigger cities, especially in tourist areas, you'll find laundry shops on the street, where the rate is usually around 10,000đ per kilo.

Mail

Mail can take anything from four days to four weeks in or out of Vietnam, depending largely where you are. Services are quickest and most reliable from the major towns, where eight to ten days is the norm. Overseas postal rates are reasonable: a postcard costs 7000–8000đ, while the price of a letter is in the region of 12,000đ for the minimum weight. Express Mail Service (EMS) operates to most countries and certain destinations within Vietnam; the service cuts down delivery times substantially and the letter or parcel is automatically registered. For a minimum-weight dispatch by EMS (under 250g), you'll pay around US$30 to the UK, US$32 to the US, US$35 to Canada and US$27 to Australia.

Poste restante services are available at all main post offices. You'll need to show your passport to collect mail and will be charged a small amount per item. Mail is held for two months before being returned. To avoid misfiling, your name should be printed clearly, with the surname in capitals and underlined, and it's still worth checking under all your names, just in case. Have letters addressed to you c/o Poste Restante, GPO, town or city, province.

When sending parcels out of Vietnam, take everything to the post office unwrapped since it will be inspected for any customs liability and wrapped for you, and the whole process, including wrapping and customs inspection, will cost you upwards of 30,000đ. Pirated CDs and DVDs and any other suspect items will be seized. Surface mail is the cheapest option, with parcels taking between one and four months.

Receiving parcels is not such a good idea. Some parcels simply go astray; those that do make it are subject to thorough customs inspections, import duty and even confiscation of suspicious items – particularly printed matter, videos or cassettes. However, if you do need to collect a parcel, remember to take your passport.

Maps

The most accurate and reliable map of Vietnam is the Rough Guides Map of Vietnam, Laos and Cambodia (1:1,200,000). Other decent maps are the International Travel Map of Vietnam (1:1,000,000) or Nelles (1:1,500,000) map of Vietnam, Laos and Cambodia: both feature plans of Ho Chi Minh City and Hanoi. Alternatively, the locally produced maps you'll find on sale in all the major towns and tourist destinations in Vietnam aren't bad.

If you need more detailed coverage, if you're cycling or motorbike touring for example, there's no beating the book of maps entitled Giao Thong Duong Bo Vietnam (1:500,000) published by Ban Do Cartographic Publishing House and available in bigger bookshops in Hanoi and Ho Chi Minh City. Trouble is, it weighs about a kilo. Another good option for cyclists and bikers is the Vietnam Administrative Atlas by the same publisher, with a map of each province per page. Look out, too, for Fauna and Flora International's Vietnam Ecotourism Map (1:1,000,000). Not only is it pretty accurate, but also includes information on visiting the national parks and other areas of environmental interest.

Money

Vietnam's unit of currency is the dong, which you'll see abbreviated as "đ", "d" or "VND" after an amount. Notes come in denominations of 500đ, 1000đ, 2000đ, 5000đ, 10,000đ, 20,000đ, 50,000đ, 100,000đ,

200,000đ and 500,000đ, coins in 200đ, 500đ, 1000đ, 2000đ and 5000đ (though coins are rarely seen). In addition to the dong, the American dollar operates as a parallel, unofficial currency and it's a good idea to carry some dollars as a back-up to pay large bills. On the whole, though, it's more convenient to operate in dong, and you'll often find dong prices are slightly lower than the equivalent in dollars.

At the time of writing, the exchange rate was around 33,000đ to £1; 20,000đ to US$1; 29,000đ to 1 Euro; 21,000đ to CA$1; 22,000đ to AUS$1; and 17,000đ to NZ$1. Recently the country has been plagued by high inflation rates, so these exchange rates are liable to fluctuate. For the latest exchange rates go to Wxe.com.

Dong are not available outside Vietnam at present, so take in some small-denomination American dollars to use until you reach a bank or ATM. Most banks and exchange bureaux don't charge for changing foreign currency into dong; banks in major cities will accept euros and other major currencies, but elsewhere may only accept dollars. Some tour agents and hotels will also change money, and most jewelry shops in Vietnam will exchange dollars at a slightly better rate than the banks, but watch out for scams. Wherever you change money, ask for a mix of denominations (in remote places, bigger bills can be hard to split), and refuse really tatty banknotes, as you'll have difficulty getting anyone else to accept them.

There's also a comprehensive network of ATMs, many open 24 hours: most accept Visa, MasterCard and American Express cards issued abroad. The maximum withdrawal is two million dong at a time, with a charge of 20,000–30,000đ per transaction (in addition to whatever surcharges your own bank levies). In Hanoi and Ho Chi Minh City you'll also find ATMs operated by ANZ and HSBC. These accept a wider range of cards, including those in the Cirrus and Plus networks.

Major credit cards – Visa, MasterCard and, to a lesser extent, American Express – are accepted in Vietnam's main cities and major tourist spots. All top-level and many mid-level hotels will accept them, as will a growing number of restaurants, though some places levy surcharges of three to four percent.

Traveler's cheques are less common now that ATMs are so widespread, but can be cashed at major banks (you need your passport as ID), for a commission of up to two percent. Vietinbank generally charges the lowest rates: at the time of writing these were 0.55 percent (minimum US$1.1) when changing into dong and 1.1 percent (minimum US$2.2) into dollars or other foreign currencies. Vietcombank waives commission on American Express traveler's cheques.

Having money wired from home via MoneyGram (UK T0800 8971 8971, US T1-800 T666-3947, Wmoneygram.com) or Western Union (US T1-800 325 6000, Wwesternunion.com) is never cheap, and should be considered a last resort. It's also possible to have money wired directly from a bank or post office in your home country to a bank in Vietnam, although this has the added complication of involving two separate institutions; money wired this way normally takes two working days to arrive, and charges vary according to the amount sent.

Opening hours

Basic hours of business are 7.30–11.30am and 1.30–4.30pm, though after lunch nothing really gets going again before 2pm. The standard closing day for offices is Sunday, and many now also close on Saturdays, including most state-run banks and government offices.

Most banks tend to work Monday to Friday 8–11.30am and 1–4pm, though some stay open later in the afternoon or may forego a lunch break. In tourist centres you'll even find branches open evenings and weekends. Post offices keep much longer hours, in general staying open from 6.30am through to 9pm with no closing day. Some sub-post offices work shorter hours and close at weekends.

Shops and markets open seven days a week and in theory keep going all day, though in practice most stallholders and many private shopkeepers will take a siesta. Shops mostly stay open late into the evenings, perhaps until 8pm or beyond in the big cities.

Museums tend to close one day a week, generally on Mondays, and their core opening hours are 8–11am and 2–4pm. Temples and pagodas occasionally close for lunch but are otherwise open all week and don't close until late evening.

Telephones

Rates for international calls are very reasonable, with international direct dialing (IDD) costing around 4,000đ per minute (depending where you are calling). Using the prefix 171 reduces rates by a further 10–20 percent. The 171 service can be used from any phone, except for operator-assisted calls, mobile phones, card phones or faxes: post offices will charge a small fee for using it.

Nearly all post offices have IDD (inter-national direct dialing) facilities, and most hotels offer IDD from your room, but you'll usually be charged at least ten percent above the norm and a minimum charge of one minute even if the call goes unanswered.

If you're running short of funds, you can almost always get a "call-back" at post offices. Ask to make a minimum (1min) call abroad and remember to get the phone number of the booth you're calling from. You can then be called back directly, at a total cost to you of a one-minute international call plus a small charge for the service. It's also possible to make collect calls to certain countries; ask at the post office or call the international operator on T110.

Local calls are easy to make and are often free, though you may be charged a small fee of a few thousand dong for the service. As in many countries, public phones are turning into battered monuments to outdated technology as mobile phones become ubiquitous (there's now more than one phone per user in Vietnam). However, transport centres like airports and bus stations still maintain a few functioning machines, which accept only pre-paid phone cards, not coins. All post offices also operate a public phone service, where the cost is displayed as you speak and you pay the cashier afterwards.

In late 2008, all phone numbers in Vietnam acquired an extra digit after the area code and before the actual number, so phone numbers in Hanoi and Ho Chi Minh City now have eight digits and other towns have seven digits after the area code. For subscribers to Vietnam Post and Telecommunications (VNPT), which is over 95 percent of the country, the extra digit is 3, though subscribers to smaller service providers have added a 2, 4, 5 or 6. I have included the new digits in this Guide, though you may still see some old numbers in Vietnam itself, and many businesses have yet to update their websites.

Mobile phones

If you want to use your own mobile phone in Vietnam, the simplest – and cheapest – thing to do is to buy a SIM card and a prepaid phone card locally. Both the big phone companies, Vinaphone (Wvinaphone.com.vn) and Mobiphone (Wmobiphone.com.vn), offer English-language support and similar prices, though Vinaphone perhaps has the edge for geographical coverage (which extends pretty much nationwide). At the time of writing, Vinaphone starter kits including a SIM card cost 120,000đ (with 100,000đ worth of calls credited to your account). Further prepaid cards are available in various sizes from 100,000đ to 500,000đ. Phone calls cost slightly more than from a land line, while sending an SMS message costs 100–300đ in Vietnam and about 2,500đ internationally. However, rates are falling rapidly as more competitors enter the increasingly deregulated market.

The other, far more expensive, option is to stick with your home service-provider – though you'll need to check beforehand whether they offer international roaming services.

Time

Vietnam is seven hours ahead of London, twelve hours ahead of New York, fifteen hours ahead of Los Angeles, one hour behind Perth and three hours behind Sydney – give or take an hour or two when summer time is in operation.

Tourist information

Tourist information on Vietnam is at a premium. The Vietnamese government maintains a handful of tourist promotion offices and a smattering of accredited travel agencies around the globe, most of which can supply you with only the most general information. A better source of information, much of it based on firsthand experiences, is the internet, with numerous websites around to help you plan your visit. Some of the more useful and interesting sites are travelfish.org, a regularly-updated online guide to Southeast Asia; worldtravelguide.net, a viewer-friendly source of information on Vietnam and other countries; Wactivetravelvietnam.com, with helpful information about national parks and beaches; and Wthingsasian.com, which consists mostly of features on Asian destinations and culture.

In Vietnam itself there's a frustrating dearth of free and impartial advice. The state-run tourist offices – under the auspices of either the Vietnam National Administration of Tourism (vietnamtourism.com) or the local provincial organization – are thinly disguised tour agents, profit-making concerns which don't take kindly to being treated as information bureaux, though the official website has a lot of useful information about destinations and practicalities such as visas. In any case, Western concepts of information don't necessarily apply here – bus timetables, for example, simply don't exist. The most you're likely to get is a glossy brochure detailing their tours and affiliated hotels.

You'll generally have more luck approaching hotel staff or one of the many private tour agencies operating in all the major tourist spots, where staff have become accustomed to Westerners' demands for advice.

Another useful source of information, including restaurant and hotel listings as well as feature articles, is the growing number of English-language magazines, such as Asialife, The Word and The Guide. There's also a government-run telephone information service (T1080) with some English-speaking staff who will answer all manner of questions – if you can get through, since the lines are often busy.

Travelers with special needs

Despite the fact that Vietnam is home to so many war-wounded, few provisions are made for the disabled. This means you'll have to be pretty self-reliant. It's important to contact airlines, hotels and tour companies as far in advance as possible to make sure they can accommodate your requirements.

Getting about can be made a little easier by taking internal flights, or by renting a private car or minibus with a driver. Taxis are widely available in Hanoi, Ho Chi Minh City and other major cities. Even so, trying to cross roads with speeding traffic and negotiating the cluttered and uneven pavements – where pavements exist – pose real problems. Furthermore, few buildings are equipped with ramps and lifts.

When it comes to accommodation, Vietnam's new luxury hotels usually offer one or two specially adapted rooms. Elsewhere, the best you can hope for is a ground-floor room, or a hotel with a lift.

One, albeit expensive, option is to ask a tour agent to arrange a customized tour. Saigontourist (saigontourist.com) has experience of running tours specifically for disabled visitors.

Traveling with children

Travelling through Vietnam with children can be challenging and fun. The Vietnamese adore kids and make a huge fuss of them, with fair-haired kids coming in for even more manhandling. The main concern will probably be hygiene: Vietnam can be distinctly unsanitary, and children's stomachs tend to be more sensitive to bacteria. Avoiding spicy foods will help while their stomachs adjust, but if children do become sick it's crucial to keep up their fluid intake, so as to avoid dehydration. Bear in mind, too, that healthcare facilities are fairly basic outside Hanoi and Ho Chi Minh City, so make sure your travel insurance includes full medical evacuation.

Long bus journeys are tough on young children, so wherever possible, take the train – at least the kids can get up and move about in safety. There are reduced fares for children on domestic flights, trains and open-tour buses. On trains, for example, it's free for under-fives (as long as they sit on your lap) and half-price for children aged five to ten. Open-tour buses follow roughly the same policy, though children paying a reduced fare are not entitled to a seat; if you don't want them on your lap you'll have to pay full fare. Tours are usually either free or half-price for children.

Many budget hotels have rooms with three or even four single beds in them. At more expensive hotels under-twelves can normally stay free of charge in their parents' rooms and baby cots are becoming more widely available.

Working and studying in Vietnam

Without a prearranged job and work permit, don't bank on finding work in Vietnam. With specific skills to offer, you could try approaching some of the Western companies now operating in Hanoi and Ho Chi Minh City.

Otherwise, English-language teaching is probably the easiest job to land, especially if you have a TEFL (Teaching English as a Foreign Language), TESOL (Teacher of English to Speakers of Other Languages) or CELTA (Certificate in English Language Teaching to Adults) qualification. Universities are worth approaching, though pay is better at private schools, where qualified teachers earn upwards of $20 an hour. In either case, you'll need to apply for a work permit, sponsored by your employer, and then a working visa. Private tutoring is an unwieldy way of earning a crust, as you'll have to pop out of the country every few months to procure a new visa. Furthermore, the authorities are clamping down on people working without the proper authorizations.

The main English-language teaching operations recruiting in Vietnam include the British Council (britishcouncil.org/Vietnam.htm), ILA Vietnam (ilavietnam.com), Language Link Vietnam (languagelink.edu.vn) and RMIT International University (rmit.edu.vn). The TEFL website (tefl.com) and Dave's ESL Café (eslcafe.com) also have lists of English-teaching vacancies in addition to lots of other useful information.

There are also opportunities for volunteer work. Try contacting the organizations listed below, or look on the websites of the NGO Resource Centre Vietnam (ngocentre.org.vn) and Volunteer Abroad (volunteerabroad.com).

Hanoi

Vietnam's capital races to make up for time lost to the ravages of war and a government that as recently as the 1990s kept the outside world at bay. Its streets surge with scooters vying for right of way amid the din of constantly blaring horns, and all around layers of history reveal periods of French and Chinese occupation – offering a glimpse into the resilience of ambitious, proud Hanoians.

Negotiate a passage past the ubiquitous knock-off merchants and you'll find the original streets of the Old Quarter. Defiant real-deal farmers hawk their wares, while city folk breakfast on noodles, practice tai chi at dawn on the shores of Hoan Kiem Lake, or play chess with goateed grandfathers.

Dine on the wild and wonderful at every corner, sample market wares, uncover an evolving arts scene, then sleep soundly in a little luxury for very little cost. Meet the people, delve into the past and witness the awakening of a Hanoi on the move.

Hanoi has shrugged off its hostile war-torn image to emerge as one of Southeast Asia's best and most culturally significant cities. There are countless museums, all offering visitors a chance to better understand Vietnam's history of revolution, war and art, while the tangled web of streets in the historic Old Quarter are a great place to wander around. It's a great launching pad for trips into Sapa and Halong Bay.

Typical Costs

Hostel prices: Dorms start at 55,000 VND while private rooms are between 218,000 – 430,000 VND for a double.

Budget hotel prices: Private rooms average 325,000 – 650,000 VND for a double.

Average cost of food: Street food is delicious and extremely cheap, with many dishes for less than 16,000 VND. 85,000 VND is enough for a meal in a casual restaurant.

Transportation costs: Bus fares are usually no more than 1,000 VND and taxis start at 19,000 VND for the first two kilometers then 12,000 VND per kilometer thereafter.

Money Saving Tips

Eat from street stalls – For the cheapest food in the city head to the Old Quarter which is packed with low-cost eats at the street stalls.

Negotiate – You should barter for everything from street stalls, markets and taxis. Tourists are often quoted huge prices and bargaining is expected.

Take the bus – These are the cheapest and most hassle-free way of getting around the city and are comfortable and efficient.

Drink Bia Hoi – This draft beer is available on the street throughout Hanoi and starts at merely 3,000 VND per glass.

Top things to see and do in Hanoi

Wander around Hoan Kiem Lake – Get here early in the morning to watch throngs of people practicing Tai Chi, running, cycling and walking before their working day begins. In the center of the lake is the Tortoise Pagoda, a shrine to the famous giant turtles that live in the lake. The lake is very beautiful and there is a temple worth visiting on the north end of the lake.

Visit the Vietnam National Museum of Fine Arts – The Fine Arts Museum is a must-see if you are interested in the various styles of Vietnamese art. There are fantastic exhibits of Buddhist art, folk art and silk and lacquer paintings but the museum's most impressive feature is Kouan Yin, the goddess of mercy who is depicted with a thousand arms and eyes.

See Quan Su Pagoda – As the headquarters for the Vietnam Central Buddhist Congregation, Quan Su is one of the most important temples in the country. If you're going to visit any of Vietnam's pagodas, this 15th century one is the one you should see.

Visit One Pillar Pagoda – Built in 1049, One-Pillar Pagoda sits on stilts over a lake and is a miniature reproduction of the original temple built by the Ly Dynasty. A prayer at this little wooden pagoda is said to bring fertility and good health.

Pay your respects at Ho Chi Minh Museum & Mausoleum – Ho Chi Minh is Vietnam's leader and founder of the communist state. Ho lies in state at this grey concrete mausoleum, which is not far from the museum dedicated to his life and belongings and the house he used to live in. You're able to walk through and see his embalmed body when it is not being repaired in Moscow. It's morbid and fascinating at the same time.

Tour Hoa Lo Prison – U.S. POWs named Hao Lo "the Hanoi Hilton" and this is where many U.S. soldiers were tortured. Sen. John McCain from Arizona is its most famous prisoner. What remains of the building is a small museum, complete with the guillotine used to execute detainees. Again, morbid but interesting.

Shop at Dong Xuan Market – Hanoi's oldest market is located in the Old Quarter. The market is multi-storied and sells everything you could ever expect, especially a lot of knock offs. The market is a bit of a Hanoi institution and probably the best place for low-cost shopping in the city.

Wander around the Old Quarter – The Old Quarter's 2,000-year-old streets are a web of shopping opportunities and cheap eateries. Gold and silver jewelry, clothes, cosmetics and even musical instruments can all be bought here alongside a myriad of other goods. There's also a lot of fascinating old worn French architecture around and you can still see the strong French influence in the area. I never bought anything but I found the chaos, the crowds, and the maze of streets fascinating to witness.

Go to the Army Museum – References to Vietnam's tumultuous history of combat are everywhere in Hanoi and a visit to the Army Museum is a good way to bring it all together. The museum has an excellent collection of planes, tanks and guns supplied by the Chinese and Soviet armies, alongside dozens of captured French and US made war machinery.

Visit the Temple of Literature – Built in 1070, the Van Mieu temple is a great example of traditional Vietnamese architecture and is one of the oldest structures in the country. Originally dedicated to Confucius, what remains today of ancient Vietnam's center of learning is five courtyards decorated with stelae which served as diplomas for the universities first doctorate students.

Learn some women's history – The problem with written history is that so much of it revolves around men, and female contributions tend to fall to the wayside. The Vietnam Women's Museum tries to turn this around with exhibits about the history and daily lives of women in Vietnamese society. There is some great material to encounter here, as well as some video interviews that will give you better insight into the life of a female street vendor.

Watch a water puppet show – Water Puppetry as an art form dates back over a millennium in Vietnam. Near the lake you can take in a show at the Water Puppet Theatre. Puppets are carved from wood, and the shows are performed in a waist-deep pool, which makes the puppets look like they're walking in water. This is a very unique and worthwhile cultural experience.

Explore the Museum of Ethnology – The Vietnamese Museum of Ethnology is a multipurpose institution, serving as both a research facility and a public museum. It contains exhibits on the different ethnic groups which reside in the country, and will give you a much better understanding of Vietnamese history.

Vietnamese Women's Museum

Address
36 P Ly Thuong Kiet, Hanoi, Vietnam

Telephone
+84 4 3825 9936

More information
www.baotangphunu.org.vn

Prices
Admission 30,000d

Opening hours
8am-5pm

This excellent, modern museum showcases women's role in
Vietnamese society and culture. Labelled in English and French, it's
the memories of the wartime contribution by individual heroic women
that are most poignant. There is a stunning collection of propaganda
posters, as well as costumes, tribal basket ware and fabric motifs from

Vietnam's ethnic minority groups. Check the website for special exhibitions.

Vietnam Museum of Ethnology

Address
Đ Nguyen Van Huyen, Hanoi, Vietnam

Telephone
+84 4 3756 2193

More information
www.vme.org.vn

Prices
adult/concession 40,000/15,000d, guide 100,000d

Opening hours
8.30am - 5.30pm Tue-Sun

This fabulous collection relating to Vietnam's ethnic minorities features well-presented tribal art, artefacts and everyday objects gathered from across the nation, and examples of traditional village houses. Displays are well labelled in Vietnamese, French and English. If you're into anthropology, it's well worth the approximately 200,000d each-way taxi fares to the Cau Giay district, about 7km from the city center, where the museum is located.

Local bus 14 (4000d) departs from P Dinh Tien Hoang on the east side of Hoan Kiem Lake and passes within a couple of blocks (around 600m) of the museum – get off at the Nghia Tan bus stop and head to Đ Nguyen Van Huyen.

Temple of Literature

Address
P Quoc Tu Giam, Hanoi, Vietnam

Telephone
+84 4 4 3845 2917

Prices
adult/student 30,000/15,000d

Opening hours
8am-5pm

Founded in 1070 by Emperor Ly Thanh Tong, the Temple of Literature is dedicated to Confucius (Khong Tu). Inside you'll find a pond known as the 'Well of Heavenly Clarity', a low-slung pagoda and statues of Confucius and his disciples. A rare example of well-preserved traditional Vietnamese architecture, the complex honors Vietnam's finest scholars and men of literary accomplishment. It is the site of Vietnam's first university, established here in 1076, when entrance was only granted to those of noble birth.

After 1442 a more egalitarian approach was adopted and gifted students from all over the nation headed to Hanoi to study the principles of Confucianism, literature and poetry. In 1484 Emperor Ly Thanh Tong ordered that stelae be erected to record the names, places of birth and achievements of exceptional scholars: 82 of 116 stelae remain standing. Paths lead from the imposing tiered gateway on P Quoc Tu Giam through formal gardens to the Khue Van pavilion, constructed in 1802.

Ho Tay

The city's largest lake, known as both Ho Tay and West Lake, is 15km in circumference and ringed by upmarket suburbs, including the predominantly expat Tay Ho district. On the south side, along Đ Thuy Khue, are seafood restaurants, and to the east, the Xuan Dieu strip is lined with restaurants, cafes, boutiques and luxury hotels. A pathway circles the lake, making for a great bicycle ride.

Hoan Kiem Lake

Legend claims in the mid-15th century Heaven sent Emperor Ly Thai To a magical sword, which he used to drive the Chinese from Vietnam. After the war a giant golden turtle grabbed the sword and disappeared into the depths of this lake to restore the sword to its divine owners, inspiring the name Ho Hoan Kiem (Lake of the Restored Sword). Every morning at around 6am local residents practice traditional tai chi on the shore.

The ramshackle Thap Rua, on an islet near the southern end, is topped with a red star and is often used as an emblem of Hanoi.

Long Bien Bridge

A symbol of the tenacity and resilience of the Hanoian people, the Long Bien Bridge (built between 1899 and 1902) was bombed on several occasions during the American War, and on each, quickly repaired by the Vietnamese. Designed by Gustave Eiffel (of Eiffel Tower fame) the bridge, used by trains, mopeds and pedestrians, is undergoing reconstruction to restore its original appearance. It's colorfully illuminated at night.

Lotte Tower Observation Deck

Address
54 Lieu Giai, Ba Dinh, Hanoi, Vietnam

Telephone
+84 4 3333 6016

More information

www.lottecenter.com.vn/eng/observation/visit_information.asp

Prices
adult/concession day 230,000/170,000d, night 130,000/110,000d

Opening hours
9am-10pm

The city's best views can be found on the 65th floor of the landmark
Lotte building, opened in 2014, in the western corner of Hanoi's Ba
Dinh district. From this uninterrupted vantage point, high above
Hanoi's hustle and bustle, one can consider the size of the Old Quarter
relative to the sheer scale of Hanoi's voracious growth. The tower also
houses a hotel, all manner of restaurants, a rooftop bar and a
department store on its lower floors.

Lotte Tower is around 20 minutes by taxi to the Old Quarter.

Ho Chi Minh City

Ho Chi Minh City, or Saigon as it is still sometimes called, is Vietnam's largest and most chaotic city. I love the chaos here, though you need to be careful (and patient) when walking across the street! Motorbikes, bicycles, cars, and rickshaws go wherever and whenever they please. It's a city with a billion things happening at once. There is a lot of information here about the war, from the War Remnants Museum to the Cu Chi Tunnels. There's a great historical museum here, though the English translation leaves a lot to be desired. The city has a lot to offer: great shops, fantastic nightlife, and delicious food.

Ho Chi Minh City (HCMC) is Vietnam at its most dizzying: a high-octane city of commerce and culture that has driven the country forward with its pulsating energy. A chaotic whirl, the city breathes life and vitality into all who settle here, and visitors cannot help but be hauled along for the ride.

From the finest of hotels to the cheapest of guesthouses, the classiest of restaurants to the tastiest of street stalls, the choicest of boutiques to the scrum of the markets, HCMC is a city of energy and discovery.

Wander through timeless alleys to incense-infused temples before negotiating chic designer malls beneath sleek 21st-century skyscrapers. The ghosts of the past live on in buildings that one generation ago witnessed a city in turmoil, but now the real beauty of the former Saigon's urban collage is the seamless blending of these two worlds into one exciting mass.

Typical Costs

Hostel prices – Low-cost dorm beds cost around 65,000–200,000 VND, while private rooms are around 220,000–650,000 VND for a double room. A great hostel (though a bit more expensive at 300,000 VND) in this city is called The Common Room Project in district 5.

Budget hotel prices – A night in a budget hotel starts at 130,000 VND, but 260,000–650,000 VND is the norm.

Average cost of food – Eat the local food and you can get a meal for around 20,000 VND. Sit down restaurants are also inexpensive at around 80,000 VND. A western burger might cost around 40,000 VND. The backpacker area, Pham Ngu Lao, has a wide range of restaurants (at varying costs for foreigners) too.

Transportation costs – Public buses around the city cost 3,500 VND. Taxis are more expensive (but still affordable) at 12,000 VND for the first kilometer and 10,000 VND per kilometer thereafter. Grabbing a taxi from the airport to the center of the city should take about 30-minutes and cost less than 200,000 VND. Motorbike taxis are also available, but aren't much cheaper than taxis, so if you're more than one person, I'd opt for a taxi.

Money Saving Tips

Taxis – Make sure the taxi drivers turn on their meter, otherwise, taxi drivers can rip you off. Or better yet, skip them and walk. Or rent a bike and try to navigate the chaos of the city.

Be ready for market sellers – When shopping in any of the city's markets you may feel like a wallet on legs as the traders call out to you. Be firm and be ready to walk away.

Eat street food – Street food in Ho Chi Minh City is inexpensive and delicious. Be sure to try a banh mi, a Vietnamese sandwich popular in the south. You can find many different kinds of noodle soup at small street stalls.

Enjoy Happy Hour – The bars in the Pham Ngu Lao area have plenty of Happy Hour drink specials, from half-price drinks to dollar cocktails, to buy one get 2 free!

Top things to do in Ho Chi Minh City

Crawl through the Cu Chi Tunnels – Crawl through the extensive network of nearly 500km of tunnels utilized by the Viet Cong in the 1960s to fight American soldiers. Tours involve a description and tour of the tunnels. It's a sobering experience and not one meant for anyone claustrophobic. However, if you want to better understand the terror of the Vietnam War, this is a must-visit.

Get lost in Chinatown – Chinatown is a hive of activity; it is a maze of temples, restaurants, jade ornaments, and medicine shops. Aside from the sprawling Binh Tay Market, you'll find some fascinating temples in the area including the Chinese Chua Quan Am Temple and Cha Tam, which is a Catholic cathedral.

Visit the Museum of Ho Chi Minh City – Not to be confused with the "Ho Chi Minh Museum," at one point or another, the city museum has been a Governor's Palace, committee building and Revolutionary Museum. Nowadays, its picturesque grounds attract newlyweds posing for photographs. You'll find a collection of weaponry and memorabilia from the country's revolutionary struggle as well as captured U.S. fighter planes and tanks.

Check out the Vietnam History Museum – The History Museum is a great place to learn about the colorful events of Vietnam's past. The museum houses a fantastic collection of ceramics, weaponry and cannons. There are photographs, clothes and household objects that date back as far as the 1700s. The English translations leave a lot to be desired though.

See the Emperor Jade Pagoda – Emperor Jade is one of the most impressive pagodas in Vietnam. The intricate carvings and depictions of deities including the Emperor Jade himself.

Admire the Notre Dame Cathedral – The Notre Dame Cathedral is an imposing red brick building built between 1877 and 1883. The two towers in the front of the cathedral rise above visitors at nearly 58 meters tall while the neon-lit statue of the Virgin Mary is also an arresting site.

Visit the War Remnants Museum – The War Remnants Museum is a must-see for anyone with an interest in Vietnam's history of combat with both the French and the Americans. Inside you'll find informative exhibits focusing on biological warfare, weaponry and in-depth statistics of Vietnam's armies during the conflicts. The museum's best exhibit is the collection of bombs, tanks, planes and war machinery, which can be found in the courtyard. The museum has a very pro-communist, down-with-the-capitalist-pigs bent to it and it's interesting to see. It's as much propaganda as it is history. Entrance fee is 15,000 VND per person.

See the Cao Dai Holy See Temple – The Cao Dai religion is relatively new at less than 100 years old. The "all-seeing eye" which dominates the architecture distinguishes the temples. This Cao Dai temple is the main temple for the religion and is hugely ornate and impressive. Most people combine a trip to the temple with the Cu Chi Tunnels excursion.

Shop at the Ben Thanh Market – Though the market is crowded and rife with pickpockets, it is the ideal place to pick up a bargain or try some traditional (and inexpensive) Vietnamese food. It's an ideal shopping place.

Escape to Can Gio Island – The Can Gio Island is popular with tourists and Ho Chi Minh locals as a way to escape the chaos of the city. The beaches here aren't mind-blowing like they are in Thailand but it's a great place to relax and one of Vietnam's better islands. The island's monkey sanctuary and mangroves are great for wildlife fans.

Ascend the Saigon Skydeck – For a 360-degree panorama of the city, you can head to the Saigon Skydeck Tower. The observation deck is on the 49th floor and entrance costs 200,000 VND (kids and seniors for 130,000 VND).

Unwind in the Twenty-Three September Park – In the hours just preceding and just after the working day, this park is packed with people exercising and playing games. Watch a Tai Chi class, play a game of badminton, or chat with one of the many students who hang out in the area.

War Remnants Museum

Address
28 Đ Vo Van Tan
cnr Đ Le Quy Don
Ho Chi Minh City, Vietnam

Telephone
+84 8 3930 5587

More information
www.baotangchungtichchientranh.vn

Prices
admission 15,000d

Opening hours
7.30am-noon & 1.30-5pm

Formerly the Museum of Chinese and American War Crimes, the War Remnants Museum is consistently popular with Western tourists. Few museums anywhere convey the brutality of war and its civilian victims. Many of the atrocities documented here were well-publicized but rarely do Westerners hear the victims of US military action tell their own stories. While some displays are one-sided, many of the most disturbing photographs illustrating US atrocities are from US sources, including those of the infamous My Lai Massacre.

US armored vehicles, artillery pieces, bombs and infantry weapons are on display outside. One corner of the grounds is devoted to the notorious French and South Vietnamese prisons on Phu Quoc and Con Son Islands. Artefacts include that most iconic of French appliances, the guillotine, and the notoriously inhumane 'tiger cages' used to house Viet Cong (Vietnamese Communists; VC) prisoners.

The ground floor of the museum is devoted to a collection of posters and photographs showing support for the antiwar movement internationally. This somewhat upbeat display provides a counterbalance to the horrors upstairs.

Even those who supported the war are likely to be horrified by the photos of children affected by US bombing and napalming. You'll also have the rare chance to see some of the experimental weapons used in the war, which were at one time military secrets, such as the flechette, an artillery shell filled with thousands of tiny darts.

Upstairs, look out for the Requiem Exhibition. Compiled by legendary war photographer Tim Page, this striking collection documents the work of photographers killed during the course of the conflict, on both sides, and includes works by Larry Burrows and Robert Capa.

The War Remnants Museum is in the former US Information Service building. Captions are in Vietnamese and English.

Notre Dame Cathedral

Address
Đ Han Thuyen
Ho Chi Minh City, Vietnam

Opening hours
Mass 9.30am Sun

Built between 1877 and 1883, Notre Dame Cathedral enlivens the heart of Ho Chi Minh City's government quarter, facing Đ Dong Khoi. A brick, neo-Romanesque church with 40m-high square towers tipped with iron spires, the Catholic cathedral is named after the Virgin Mary. Interior walls are inlaid with devotional tablets and some stained glass survives. English-speaking staff dispense tourist information from 9am to 11am Monday to Saturday. If the front gates are locked, try the door on the side facing the Reunification Palace.

Jade Emperor Pagoda

Address
73 Đ Mai Thi Luu
Ho Chi Minh City, Vietnam

Opening hours
7am-6pm, on 1st & 15th of lunar month 5am-7pm

Built in 1909 in honor of the supreme Taoist god (the Jade Emperor or King of Heaven, Ngoc Hoang), this is one of the most spectacularly atmospheric temples in Ho Chi Minh City, stuffed with statues of phantasmal divinities and grotesque heroes. The pungent smoke of incense (huong) fills the air, obscuring the exquisite woodcarvings. Its roof encrusted with elaborate tile work, the temple's statues, depicting characters from both Buddhist and Taoist lore, are made from reinforced papier mâché.

Inside the main building are two especially fierce and menacing Taoist figures. On the right (as you face the altar) is a 4m-high statue of the general who defeated the Green Dragon (depicted underfoot).

On the left is the general who defeated the White Tiger, which is also being stepped on.

Worshippers mass before the ineffable Jade Emperor, who presides – draped in luxurious robes and shrouded in a dense fog of incense smoke – over the main sanctuary. He is flanked by his guardians, the Four Big Diamonds (Tu Dai Kim Cuong), so named because they are said to be as hard as diamonds.

Out the door on the left-hand side of the Jade Emperor's chamber is another room. The semi-enclosed area to the right (as you enter) is presided over by Thanh Hoang, the Chief of Hell; to the left is his red horse. Other figures here represent the gods who dispense punishments for evil acts and rewards for good deeds. The room also contains the famous Hall of the Ten Hells, carved wooden panels illustrating the varied torments awaiting evil people in each of the Ten Regions of Hell. Women queue up at the seated effigy of the City God, who wears a hat inscribed with Chinese characters that announce 'At one glance, money is given'. In a mesmerizing ritual, worshippers first put money into a box, then rub a piece of red paper against his hand before circling it around a candle flame.

On the other side of the wall is a fascinating little room in which the ceramic figures of 12 women, overrun with children and wearing colorful clothes, sit in two rows of six. Each of the women exemplifies a human characteristic, either good or bad (as in the case of the woman drinking alcohol from a jug). Each figure represents a year in the 12-year Chinese astrological calendar. Presiding over the room is Kim Hoa Thanh Mau, the Chief of All Women. Upstairs is a hall to Quan Am, the Goddess of Mercy, opposite a portrait of Dat Ma, the bearded Indian founder of Zen Buddhism.

The multi-faith nature of the temple is echoed in the shrine's alternative name Phuoc Hai Tu (福海寺; Sea of Blessing Temple), whose message is clearly Buddhist. Similarly, the Chinese characters (佛光普照; Phat Quang Pho Chieu) in the main temple hall mean 'The light of Buddha shines on all'.

Outside, a small pond seethes with turtles, some of which have shells inscribed with auspicious inscriptions.

Binh Tay Market

Address
57a ĐL Thap Muoi
Ho Chi Minh City, Vietnam

More information
www.chobinhtay.gov.vn

Cholon's main market has a great clock tower and a central courtyard with gardens. Much of the business here is wholesale but it's popular with tour groups. The market was originally built by the French in the 1880s; Guangdong-born philanthropist Quach Dam paid for its rebuilding and was commemorated by a statue that is now in the Fine

Arts Museum. Expect a friendly welcome when you sit down for breakfast or coffee with the market's street food vendors.

Central Post Office

Address
2 Cong Xa Paris
Ho Chi Minh City, Vietnam

Right across the way from Notre Dame Cathedral, Ho Chi Minh City's striking French post office is a period classic, designed by Gustave Eiffel and built between 1886 and 1891. Painted on the walls of its grand concourse are fascinating historic maps of South Vietnam, Saigon and Cholon, while a mosaic of Ho Chi Minh takes pride of place at the end of its barrel-vaulted hall. Note the magnificent tiled floor of the interior and the copious green-painted wrought iron.

Bitexco Financial Tower

Address
2 Đ Hai Trieu
Ho Chi Minh City, Vietnam

More information
www.saigonskydeck.com

Prices
adult/children 200,000/130,000d

Opening hours
9.30am-9.30pm

The 68-storey, 262m-high, Carlos Zapata–designed skyscraper dwarfs all around it. It's reportedly shaped like a lotus bulb, but also resembles a CD rack with a tambourine shoved into it. That tambourine is the 48th-floor Saigon Skydeck, with a helipad on its roof. Choose a clear day and aim for sunset (or down a drink in the Eon Heli Bar instead).

Hoi An

Graceful, historic Hoi An is Vietnam's most atmospheric and delightful town. Once a major port, it boasts the grand architecture and beguiling riverside setting that befits its heritage, but the 21st-century curses of traffic and pollution are almost entirely absent.

Hoi An owes its easygoing provincial demeanor and remarkably harmonious old-town character more to luck than planning. Had the Thu Bon River not silted up in the late 19th century – so ships could no longer access the town's docks – Hoi An would doubtless be very different today. For a century, the city's allure and importance dwindled until an abrupt rise in fortunes in the 1990s, when a tourism boom transformed the local economy. Today Hoi An is once again a cosmopolitan melting pot, one of the nation's m o st wealthy towns, a culinary mecca and one of Vietnam's most important tourism centres.

This revival of fortunes has preserved the face of the Old Town and its incredible legacy of tottering Japanese merchant houses, Chinese temples and ancient tea warehouses – though, of course, residents and rice fields have been gradually replaced by tourist businesses. Lounge bars, boutique hotels, travel agents and a glut of tailor shops are very much part of the scene here. And yet, down by the market and over on Cam Nam Island, you'll find life has changed little. Travel a few kilometers further – you'll find some superb bicycle, motorbike and boat trips – and some of central Vietnam's most enticingly laidback scenery and beaches are within easy reach.

The town is packed with picturesque historical homes, pagodas and street-side cafes. The place is extremely popular for buying clothes. You can get anything made here – from custom-made suits to gowns to sundresses to leather boots to sneakers. But even if you don't want to shop, Hoi An makes for a relaxing destination in an otherwise frenetic country, after all, a day at the beach is only a bike-ride out of town.

Tan Ky House

Address
101 Đ Nguyen Thai Hoc
Hoi An, Vietnam

Prices
admission by Old Town ticket

Opening hours
8am-noon & 2-4.30pm

Built two centuries ago by an ethnically Vietnamese family, this gem of a house has been lovingly preserved through seven generations. Look out for signs of Japanese and Chinese influences on the architecture. Japanese elements include the ceiling (in the sitting area), which is supported by three progressively shorter beams, one on top of the other. Under the crab-shell ceiling are carvings of crossed sabers wrapped in silk ribbon. The sabers symbolize force; the silk represents flexibility.

The interior is brightened by a beautiful detail: Chinese poems written in inlaid mother-of-pearl hang from some of the columns that hold up the roof. The Chinese characters on these 150-year-old panels are formed entirely of birds gracefully portrayed in various positions of flight.

The courtyard has several functions: to let in light, provide ventilation, bring a glimpse of nature into the home, and collect rainwater and provide drainage. The carved wooden balcony supports around the courtyard are decorated with grape leaves, which are a European import and further evidence of the unique blending of cultures in Hoi An.

The back of the house faces the river and was rented out to foreign merchants. Marks on one wall record recent flood heights, including the 1964 record when the water covered almost the entire ground level. There are two pulleys attached to a beam in the loft – in the past they were used for moving goods into storage, and today for raising furniture for safekeeping from the floods.

The exterior of the roof is made of tiles; inside, the ceiling consists of wood. This design keeps the house cool in summer and warm in winter.

Assembly Hall of the Fujian Chinese Congregation

Address
opposite 35 Đ Tran Phu
Hoi An, Vietnam

Prices
admission by Old Town ticket

Opening hours
7am-5.30pm

Originally a traditional assembly hall, this structure was later transformed into a temple for the worship of Thien Hau, a deity from

Fujian province. The green-tiled triple gateway dates from 1975. The mural on the right-hand wall depicts Thien Hau, her way lit by lantern light as she crosses a stormy sea to rescue a foundering ship. Opposite is a mural of the heads of the six Fujian families who fled from China to Hoi An in the 17th century.

The penultimate chamber contains a statue of Thien Hau. To either side of the entrance stand red-skinned Thuan Phong Nhi and green-skinned Thien Ly Nhan, deities who alert Thien Hau when sailors are in distress.

In the last chamber, the central altar contains seated figures of the heads of the six Fujian families. The smaller figures below them represent their successors as clan leaders. Behind the altar on the right are three fairies and smaller figures representing the 12 ba mu (midwives), each of whom teaches newborns a different skill necessary for the first year of life: smiling, sucking and so forth. Childless couples often come here to pray for offspring and leave fresh fruit as offerings.

Japanese Covered Bridge

This beautiful little bridge is emblematic of Hoi An. A bridge was first constructed here in the 1590s by the Japanese community to link them with the Chinese quarters. Over the centuries the ornamentation has remained relatively faithful to the original Japanese design. The French flattened out the roadway for cars, but the original arched shape was restored in 1986.

The structure is very solidly constructed because of the threat of earthquakes. The entrances to the bridge are guarded by weathered statues: a pair of monkeys on one side, a pair of dogs on the other. According to one story, many of Japan's emperors were born in the years of the dog and monkey. Another tale says that construction of the bridge started in the year of the monkey and was finished in the year of the dog. The stelae, listing all Vietnamese and Chinese contributors to a subsequent restoration of the bridge, are written in chu nho (Chinese characters) – the nom script had not yet become popular. While access to the Japanese Bridge is free, you have to surrender a ticket to see a small, unimpressive temple built into the bridge's northern side.

Tran Family Chapel

Address
21 Đ Le Loi
Hoi An, Vietnam

Prices
admission by Old Town ticket

Opening hours
7.30am-noon & 2-5.30pm

Built for worshipping family ancestors, this chapel dates back to 1802. It was commissioned by Tran Tu, one of the clan who ascended to the rank of mandarin and served as an ambassador to China. His picture is to the right of the chapel. The architecture of the building reflects the influence of Chinese (the 'turtle' style roof), Japanese (triple beam) and vernacular (look out for the bow-and-arrow detailing) styles.

The central door is reserved for the dead – it's opened at Tet and on 11 November, the death anniversary of the main ancestor. Traditionally, women entered from the left and men from the right, although these distinctions are no longer observed.

The wooden boxes on the altar contain the Tran ancestors' stone tablets, with chiseled Chinese characters setting out the dates of birth and death, along with some small personal effects. On the anniversary of each family member's death, their box is opened, incense is burned and food is offered.

After a short tour, you'll be shown to the 'antique' room, where there are lots of coins for sale, and a side room full of souvenirs.

Quan Cong Temple

Address
24 Đ Tran Phu
Hoi An, Vietnam

Prices
admission by Old Town ticket

Founded in 1653, this small temple is dedicated to Quan Cong, an esteemed Chinese general who is worshipped as a symbol of loyalty, sincerity, integrity and justice. His partially gilded statue, made of papier-mâché on a wooden frame, is on the central altar at the back of the sanctuary. When someone makes an offering to the portly looking Quan Cong, the caretaker solemnly strikes a bronze bowl that makes a bell-like sound.

On the left of Quan Cong is a statue of General Chau Xuong, one of his guardians, striking a tough-guy pose. On the right is the rather plump administrative mandarin Quan Binh. The life-sized white horse recalls a mount ridden by Quan Cong.

Check out the carp-shaped rain spouts on the roof surrounding the courtyard. The carp is a symbol of patience in Chinese mythology and is popular in Hoi An.

Shoes should be removed when mounting the platform in front of the statue of Quan Cong.

Hoi An Old Town

More information
www.hoianworldheritage.org.vn

Prices
tickets 120,000d

By Unesco decree, more than 800 historical buildings in Hoi An have been preserved, so much of the Old Town looks as it did several centuries ago. Eighteen of these buildings are open to visitors and require an Old Town ticket for admission; the fee goes towards funding conservation work.

Each ticket allows you to visit five different heritage attractions: museums, assembly halls, ancient houses and a traditional music show at the Handicraft Workshop. Tickets are valid for 10 days.

The Chinese who settled in Hoi An identified themselves according to their province of origin. Each community built its own assembly hall, known as hoi quan in Vietnamese, for social gatherings, meetings and celebrations.

All the old houses, except Diep Dong Nguyen and Quan Thang, offer short guided tours. They are efficient, if a tad perfunctory.

Nha Trang

Nha Trang is the popular beach destination for people in Vietnam. White, sandy beaches are imposed against a dramatic backdrop of mountains, and with nineteen islands to choose from, it is no wonder that this is a popular place for tourists. This is the perfect spot to learn how to dive, while still keeping your budget in check. While the beaches are nice, keep in mind this place is very, very popular and can sometimes be a bit of a hassle or full of drunk backpackers.

The high-rise, high-energy beach resort of Nha Trang enjoys a stunning setting: ringed by a necklace of hills, with a sweeping crescent beach, the city's turquoise bay is dotted with tropical islands.

The shoreline has been given a huge makeover in recent years, with parks and sculpture gardens spread along the impressive promenade, while the streets inland reveal some quirky boutiques and a cosmopolitan array of dining options.

As the restaurants wind down, the nightlife cranks up – Nha Trang is a party town at heart, like any self-respecting resort should be. Forget the curfews of the capital; people play late in this town.

If cocktails and shooters aren't your flavor, there are some more sedate activities on offer. Try an old-school spa treatment with a visit to a mud bath or explore centuries-old Cham towers still standing in the center of town.

This part of the country has its very own microclimate and the rains tend to come from October until December, a time best avoided if you are into lazing on the beach or diving in the tropical waters.

Po Nagar Cham Towers

Prices
admission 22,000d, guide 50,000d

Opening hours
6am-6pm

Built between the 7th and 12th centuries, these four Cham Towers are still actively used for worship by Cham, Chinese and Vietnamese Buddhists. Originally the complex had seven or eight towers, but only four towers remain, of which the 28m-high North Tower (Thap Chinh), which dates from AD 817, with its terraced pyramidal roof, vaulted interior masonry and vestibule, is the most magnificent.

The towers stand on a granite knoll 2km north of central Nha Trang, on the banks of the Cai River.

It's thought this site was first used for worship as early as the 2nd century AD. The original wooden structure was razed to the ground by attacking Javanese in AD 774, but was replaced by a stone-and-brick temple (the first of its kind) in 784.

The towers serve as the Holy See, honoring Yang Ino Po Nagar, the goddess of the Dua (Liu) clan, which ruled over the southern part of the Cham kingdom. There are inscribed stone slabs scattered throughout the complex, most of which relate to history or religion and provide insight into the spiritual life and social structure of the Cham.

All of the temples face east, as did the original entrance to the complex, which is to the right as you ascend the hillock. In centuries past, worshippers passed through the pillared meditation hall, 10 pillars of which can still be seen, before proceeding up the steep staircase to the towers.

In 918, King Indravarman III placed a gold mukha-linga (carved phallus with a human face painted on it) in the North Tower, but it was taken by Khmer raiders. This pattern of statues being destroyed or stolen and then replaced continued until 965, when King Jaya Indravarman IV replaced the gold mukha-linga with the stone figure, Uma (shakti, or female consort of Shiva), which remains to this day.

Above the entrance to the North Tower, two musicians, one of whose feet is on the head of the bull Nandin, flank a dancing four-armed Shiva. The sandstone doorposts are covered with inscriptions, as are parts of the walls of the vestibule. A gong and a drum stand under the pyramid-shaped ceiling of the antechamber. In the 28m-high pyramidal main chamber, there is a black-stone statue of the goddess Uma with 10 arms, two of which are hidden under her vest; she is seated and leaning back against a monstrous beast.

The Central Tower (Thap Nam) was built partly of recycled bricks in the 12th century on the site of a structure dating from the 7th century. It is less finely constructed than the other towers and has little ornamentation; the pyramidal roof lacks terracing or pilasters, although the interior altars were once covered with silver. There is a linga inside the main chamber.

The South Tower (Mieu Dong Nam), at one time dedicated to Sandhaka (Shiva), still shelters a linga, while the richly ornamented Northwest Tower (Thap Tay Bac) was originally dedicated to Ganesh. To the rear of the complex is a less impressive museum with a few examples of Cham stonework.

To get here from central Nha Trang, take Đ Quang Trung (which becomes Đ 2 Thang 4) north across the Ha Ra and Xom Bong Bridges. Po Nagar can also be reached via the Tran Phu Bridge along the beachfront road.

This site has a continuing religious significance, so be sure to remove your shoes before entering.

Nha Trang Beach

Forming a magnificent sweeping arc, Nha Trang's 6km-long golden sand beach is the city's trump card. Various sections are roped-off and designated for swimmers (where you won't be bothered by jet skis or boats). The turquoise water is fabulously inviting, and the promenade a delight to stroll.

Two popular lounging spots are the Sailing Club and Louisiane Brewhouse. If you head south of here, the beach gets quieter and it's possible to find a stretch of sand to yourself.

The best beach weather is generally before 1pm, as the afternoon sea breezes can whip up the sand.

During heavy rains, run-off from the rivers at each end of the beach flows into the bay, gradually turning it a murky brown. Most of the year, however, the sea is just like it appears in the brochures.

Long Son Pagoda

Opening hours
7.30-11.30am & 1.30-5.30pm

This striking pagoda was founded in the late 19th century. The entrance and roofs are decorated with mosaic dragons constructed of glass and ceramic tile while the main sanctuary is a hall adorned with modern interpretations of traditional motifs.

Behind the pagoda is a huge white Buddha seated on a lotus blossom. Around the statue's base are fire-ringed relief busts of Thich Quang Duc and six other Buddhist monks who died in self-immolations in 1963.

The platform around the 14m-high Buddha has great views of Nha Trang and nearby rural areas. As you approach the pagoda from the street, the 152 stone steps up the hill to the Buddha begin to the right of the structure. Take some time to explore off to the left, where there's an entrance to another hall of the pagoda.

Beggars congregate within the complex, as do a number of scam artists. There's a persistent scam here, where visitors are approached by children (and adults) with pre-printed name badges claiming to work for the monks. After showing you around the pagoda, whether invited to or not, they will then demand money 'for the monks' or 'for a prayer'. If that fails, they insist that you buy postcards for 200,000d. The best course of action is to ignore them when they first appear, if they persist, tell them you're not going to give them any money. If you do want to make a contribution towards the upkeep of the complex, leave it in the donation boxes as you would in any other pagoda.

The pagoda is located about 400m west of the train station, just off Đ 23 Thang 10.

Alexandre Yersin Museum

Address

10 Đ Tran Phu
N ha Trang, Vietnam

Telephone
+84 58 382 2355

Prices
admission 26,000d

Opening hours
7.30-11am & 2-4.30pm Mon-Fri, 8-11am Sat

Highly popular in Vietnam, Dr Alexandre Yersin (1863–1943) founded Nha Trang's Pasteur Institute in 1895. He learned to speak Vietnamese fluently, introduced rubber and quinine-producing trees to Vietnam, and discovered the rat-borne microbe that causes bubonic plague.

You can see Yersin's library and office at this small, interesting museum; displays include laboratory equipment (such as astronomical instruments) and a fascinating 3-D photo viewer.

Tours are conducted in French, English and Vietnamese, and a short film on Yersin's life is shown.

Yersin travelled throughout the central highlands and recorded his observations. During this period, he came upon the site of what is now Dalat and recommended that a hill station be established there.

Today, the Pasteur Institute in Nha Trang coordinates vaccination and hygiene programs for the country's southern coastal region. The institute produces vaccines and carries out medical research and testing to European standards. Physicians at the clinic h e re offer medical advice to around 70 patients a day.

Hon Chong Promontory

Prices
admission 21,000d

The narrow granite promontory of Hon Chong offers fine views of the mountainous coastline north of Nha Trang and the nearby islands.

The beach here has a more local flavor than Nha Trang Beach (but the accompanying refuse is unpleasant). Still, it's fun to watch local kids do Acapulco-style swan dives into the ocean.

There is a reconstructed traditional Ruong residence and a great cafe. A taxi here from the city center is around 30,000d.

About 300m south of Hon Chong (towards Nha Trang) and a few dozen meters from the beach is tiny Hon Do (Red Island), which has a Buddhist temple on top. To the northeast is Hon Rua (Tortoise Island), which really does resemble a tortoise. The two islands of Hon Yen (Bird's-Nest Island) are off in the distance to the east.

Nha Trang Cathedral

Address
cnr Đ Nguyen Trai & Đ Thai Nguyen
Nha Trang, Vietnam

Built between 1928 and 1933 in French Gothic style, complete with stained-glass windows, Nha Trang Cathedral stands on a small hill overlooking the train station. It's a surprisingly elegant building given that it was constructed of simple cement blocks. Some particularly colorful Vietnamese touches include the red neon outlining the crucifix, the pink back-lighting on the tabernacle and the blue neon arch and white neon halo over the statue of St Mary.

In 1988, a Catholic cemetery not far from the church was disinterred to make room for a new railway building. The remains were brought to the cathedral and reburied in the cavities behind the wall of plaques that line the ramp up the hill.

Conclusion

Thank you for reading my book 'Vietnam Travel Guide'. I hope it will be of use to you and that you will enjoy reading it on the road in Vietnam.

If you enjoyed it, you can take a look at some of my other book which include other travel guides. You can find all of them here:
https://www.amazon.com/Alex-Pitt/e/B0184KH3EI

64030551R00116

Made in the USA
Lexington, KY
25 May 2017